Cultivating Inquiry-Driven Learners

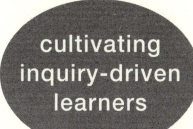

cultivating inquiry-driven learners

a college education for the 21st century

CLIFTON CONRAD and LAURA DUNEK

The Johns Hopkins University Press
Baltimore

2 4 6 8 9 7 5 3 1

The Johns Hopkins University Press
2715 North Charles Street
Baltimore, Maryland 21218-4363
www.press.jhu.edu

Library of Congress Cataloging-in-Publication Data

Conrad, Clifton.
Cultivating inquiry-driven learners : a college education for the
twenty-first century / Clifton Conrad and Laura Dunek.
    pages   cm
Includes bibliographical references and index.
ISBN 978-1-4214-0598-8 (hdbk. : alk. paper)—ISBN 978-1-4214-0599-5
(pbk. : alk. paper)—ISBN 978-1-4214-0636-7 (electronic)—
ISBN 1-4214-0598-9 (hdbk. : alk. paper)—ISBN 1-4214-0599-7 (pbk. : alk.
paper)—ISBN 1-4214-0636-5 (electronic)
    1. Education, Higher—United States.   2. Education, Humanistic—United
States.   3. Inquiry-based learning—United States.   I. Dunek, Laura.
II. Title.
    LA227.4.C66 2012
    371.3'84—dc23   2011047303

A catalog record for this book is available from the British Library.

*Special discounts are available for bulk purchases of this book. For
more information, please contact Special Sales at 410-516-6936 or
specialsales@press.jhu.edu.*

*Virginia Margaret Angell Conrad (1923–1969) and Julia
Peterson Conrad, my mother and my wife, who
remain two of the most inspiring and wonderful
human beings
I have known
—Clifton Conrad*

*For my friends and family, especially my loving husband,
Shawn David Guse, and for Martin Joseph Kemps
(1914–2006), my kind and courageous grandfather who
inspired in us all an ardent love for learning.
—Laura Dunek*

contents

Much of the world remains captivated by America's colleges and universities. Students matriculate to our institutions of higher learning from across the globe, and our universities continue to dominate the global rankings. In 2010, the Shanghai Ranking Consultancy's world ranking of universities placed 17 U.S. institutions in the top 20 universities in the world. But scarcely a decade into the twenty-first century, our colleges and universities have been catapulted into an uncertain and rapidly changing landscape that , in large measure, is tethered to the shift from a national economy driven by industrial production to a global economy driven by knowledge and innovation.

Nested in this context, a substantial body of thoughtful consideration over the past several decades has been aimed at capturing the essence of a college education. Yet, the discourse continues to be dominated by high-flying rhetoric that has fallen short of advancing a transformative and unifying purpose of a college education for the twenty-first century.

In the absence of an overarching purpose of a college education and increasingly under the influence of market forces, most colleges and universities have fallen back to a default vision of a college education: developing knowledge-inundated, workplace-educated commodities. This core emphasis on knowledge acquisition fails to recognize that in the uncertain world in which we live, individuals must first and foremost be prepared to develop ideas that will prepare them to meet the rapid and constant change that awaits them over the course of their lives. Moreover, this default purpose looks upon a college education as a "commodity," which, in effect, treats individuals as consumers rather than as human beings; emphasizes job preparation rather than cultivating the capacity of students to adapt to a constantly changing workplace in the decades to come; and places relatively little emphasis on preparing people to address both foreseen and unforeseen challenges and opportunities in their public and personal lives as well as in the workplace.

This volume is anchored in the critical need to develop an overarching and transparent purpose of a college education that can be shared across our colleges and universities. From our perspective, this purpose should accommodate the institutional diversity that has long been a hallmark of the higher learning in the United States; be responsive to the rapidly changing landscape of the twenty-first century; cut across general education and specialization, as well as fields of study ranging from the liberal arts and sciences to professional fields; and help to guide our design of undergraduate education as well as inform our teaching and learning.

In the spirit of the historic dialogues between W. E. B. DuBois and Booker T. Washington (Dunn, 1993) as well as those between John Dewey and Robert Hutchins (Dewey, 1937), while reading this book we invite stakeholders from across the field of higher learning to join us in addressing this question: If we are to help students flourish as human beings throughout their lives—what the original Greek referred to as *eudaimonia,* or "human flourishing" (Bakewell, 2010, p. 109)—what should be the fundamental purpose of a college education in the twenty-first century? We also invite stakeholders to challenge our ideas page by page, engaging themselves and others in an ongoing dialogue aimed at helping enrich the discourse on the purpose of a college education in the twenty-first century.

To that end, the book is divided into four parts. In Part One we review and reflect on the contemporary discourse on the purpose of a college education and, in turn, suggest that a fundamental purpose is conspicuously absent. In Part Two we begin by exploring the new world of the twenty-first century, including the market forces buffeting higher education within the global knowledge and information economy, and then suggest that the contemporary default purpose of a college education—the development of knowledge-inundated, workplace commodities—is already making undergraduate education obsolete. In Part Three, the centerpiece of this volume, we propose a fundamental purpose of a college education: educating inquiry-driven learners. In Part Four we provide examples of contemporary initiatives in selected colleges and universities that give expression to this purpose, both in the curriculum and in teaching and learning.

In introducing this volume, we take the liberty of reflecting on what led us to undertake this project and what inspired us throughout our journey in writing this book.

Clifton Conrad

I have long had a conflicted relationship with higher education. On the one hand, my mother and grandmother—both college-educated at highly "reputable" institutions—cultivated a sense of wonder in many of their offspring, including me, and a deep reverence for learning for its own sake. On the other hand, some members of my family viewed higher education as the securing of a credential, preferably at an Ivy League institution, that was rooted in acquiring a body of knowledge that would serve one well over the course of one's lifetime.

Fueled by a seemingly insatiable sense of curiosity and numerous opportunities—such as the opportunity as an undergraduate to spend an entire day with the political philosopher Isaiah Berlin and another day with the English writer C. P. Snow—I somehow persisted in securing proper credentials and, in turn, chose to spend my adult life as a teacher and scholar invested in the study of undergraduate and graduate education. For more than three decades, I have had the great pleasure of writing books and articles on undergraduate education—including liberal education and general education, the humanities and fine arts, and professional education.

Notwithstanding a lifetime love affair with higher education and the exhilarating rhetoric on liberal education, I have been troubled for many years by the fact that there is woefully little agreement in higher education on the purpose of a college education—and not much willingness to engage in public dialogue that is aimed at reaching some consensus on the matter. To illustrate, I invite the reader to randomly ask two professors to share their definition of the purpose of a college education and, in turn, how that definition finds expression in their teaching and learning. What are the odds that there will be more than a dollop or two of agreement between the two professors? While many proponents of liberal education celebrate the acquisition of knowledge as the core of a college education, I have become increasingly uneasy with the notion that simply acquiring a foundation of knowledge equips one for an uncertain world, in which much of the knowledge we acquire may have a shelf life of only a few years. (I once served on a panel with Mortimer Adler, a co-founder of the Great Books Foundation, whose self-appointed capacity to access "truth" convinced me that simply becoming "learned" in Western civilization would fall short of adequately "cultivating my humanity," much less my capacity to contribute to higher learning as a teacher or scholar.)

Much to my dismay, higher education has increasingly come to be viewed in our society mostly as a credential. Not only do most students and their parents celebrate college completion as the gold standard, but most higher education researchers do so as well. If a college education is to be more than a credential, we must address the question: What is the purpose of a college education? Put another way, What do we want undergraduate students to learn if they are to become "educated"?

Nearly a decade ago, while on a road trip with my wife, Julia, to Yosemite National Park, I officially launched my inquiry on the purpose of a college education for the twenty-first century. Ever since then, in my travels to colleges and universities across the globe, from Latin America and Europe to the Middle East and Asia, I have had vigorous discussions with administrators, faculty, and students about the purpose of a college education. Along with these conversations, my ongoing dialogue with the existing literature and my interactions with many faculty, students, and administrators across the United States variously informed the ideas advanced in this book. I have especially appreciated my ongoing discussions with colleagues at the University of Wisconsin–Madison, such as Professor Paul Bredeson and graduate students Erin Vander Loop, Geoffrey Mamerow, and Todd Lundberg. And, most significantly, with my co-author, Laura

Dunek, and with Julia, I have had spirited, enriching, and vigorous dialogue in the crafting of this book.

Laura Dunek

It has been an honor to join Clifton Conrad in bringing this book to fruition. Rarely does one have the opportunity to advance innovative ideas that hold the potential to profoundly benefit humankind. At present, I am a graduate student pursuing a doctoral degree at the University of Wisconsin–Madison, School of Education. This pursuit heralds the genesis of a second career for me: after serving for several years as legal counsel for the University of Wisconsin System, I determined to earn a doctorate in Educational Leadership and Policy Analysis so that I could thereafter pursue a leadership role in higher education. I was inspired to do so by my clients, all of whom are leaders in public higher education, because I consistently observed that through their vision and guidance they positively benefitted not only the communities served by their institutions but also, and most especially, the students enrolled in their colleges and universities. Suffice to say, I finally discovered that my passion in life is to serve the public good, and I cannot imagine a better way to do so than by serving in a leadership role in higher education.

My academic research focuses upon the societal and economic role of public higher education in the United States in the twenty-first century, and thus far, I am dismayed by many of the developments that I have observed. All across the country, state governments are cutting funding for public higher education in an effort to balance budgets in a time of diminished tax revenues, and the general public increasingly perceives that college degrees are a private benefit that serve graduating students, as distinguished from a public benefit, which increases tax revenues and community volunteerism, spurs the creation of start-up companies, and draws existing employers to regions where large numbers of college graduates reside.

Simultaneous to this diminished public support for higher education is a dynamically shifting U.S. economy. The emerging global economy has shifted manufacturing away from the United States to developing nations such as China and India, and an emerging knowledge and innovation economy has become a fast-growing sector of our national economy. Because universities are the wellspring of knowledge and innovation in the United States, higher education holds the potential to play an integral role in economic growth at this juncture in our nation's history. What perplexes me, however, is the disconnect between higher education's integral role in an emerging knowledge economy and in sustained economic growth, and the diminished public funding and support for higher education in the United States. Both China and India are pouring millions of dollars of additional support into their systems of public higher education, but not the United States, which leaves me asking a simple question: If it's a knowledge economy, then why are we reducing support for the very sources of knowledge and innovation that we need to succeed?

I also am concerned that both the students enrolled in institutions of higher learning and the institutions themselves are increasingly drifting away from prioritizing human development and preparation for public service. In the modern era, many public colleges and universities are moving toward corporate models that focus upon sustaining revenue, which is a rational response to diminished public funding but which also throws into question the fundamental purpose of public higher education. Moreover, at the student level I am concerned that our new generations of students are worried more about the bottom line—how to afford college and how to find a high-paying job—than they are about their own human development. But across the span of a lifetime, no one works twenty-four hours a day, seven days a week, and everyone must undergo personal development and engage in interpersonal relationships. Ought not our students focus upon more than what they will be doing during their work hours after graduation, and instead expand their college expectations to include their development as human beings and engaged members of a global society?

It is my hope that by submitting this book and its ideas into the intellectual commons, Professor Conrad and I will catalyze discussion among leaders in higher education and their students. Perhaps our work will shed light on what ought to be the fundamental purpose of a college education in the twenty-first century, and our ideas will contribute to the vitality of our colleges and universities in the unfolding millennium by helping to inform the future trajectory of American higher education.

In writing this book Clif Conrad and I frequently found ourselves inspired by this quote by Hisham Matar: "Books written out of fire give me a great deal of pleasure. You get the sense that the world for these writers could not have continued if the book hadn't been written. When you come across a book like that it is a privilege" (2007, p. 11). This book was written out of fire; whether it is a privilege for others to read and reflect on is for them to judge.

part one

What Is the Purpose of a College Education?

chapter one

Contemporary Discourse on the Purpose of a College Education

Our colleges and universities continue to be among the most widely respected institutions in the world. Jonathan Cole, in *The Great American University* (2009), recently claimed that higher learning in the United States has reached its zenith. After studying the individual and societal benefits of college, both monetary and nonmonetary, Walter McMahon (2009) reported in *Higher Learning, Greater Good* that the societal benefits are no less significant than the individual benefits. He found that a college education not only enhances job opportunities, earnings, and health for the individual, but it also promotes sustainable growth, reduces crime, and lowers state welfare costs, among other societal benefits.

Notwithstanding widespread enthusiasm for American higher education, undergraduate education in particular has received unprecedented and increasingly harsh criticism in recent years. Numerous critics have argued that colleges and universities have traded educational values for marketplace principles. For example, Wesley Shumar, in *College for Sale* (1997), attacks the commodification of higher education; David Kirp, in *Shakespeare, Einstein, and the Bottom Line* (2003), provides animated stories of the consequences of the commercialization of higher education on undergraduate education; Stanley Aronowitz, in *The Knowledge Factory* (2000), Henry Giroux, in *The University in Chains* (2007), and Marc Bousquet, in *How the University Works* (2008), argue against the corrosive effects of corporate ideology on higher learning; Christopher Newfield, in *Unmaking the Public University* (2008), argues that market forces have undercut undergraduate education at the expense of higher education's nonmarket purposes;

and Gaye Tuchman, in *Wannabe University* (2009), advances a stinging critique of the consequences of placing loyalty to the market above the cultivation of traditional educational values.

Much of the criticism has focused on the quality of undergraduate education, and includes Page Smith's *Killing the Spirit* (1990), Martin Anderson's *Imposters in the Temple* (1992), Robert Solomon and Jon Solomon's *Up the University* (1993), Richard Vedder's *Going Broke by Degrees* (2004), Ellen Schrecker's *The Lost Soul of Higher Education* (2010), and Nancy Folbre's *Saving State U* (2010). To illustrate, a recent book by Andrew Hacker and Claudia Dreifus entitled *Higher Education?* (2010) argues that our colleges and universities have lost sight of their primary mission—the education of young people. Seeming to position themselves as consumer advocates, Hacker and Dreifus's criticisms of undergraduate education echo many contemporary criticisms: the emphasis on training rather than education, mediocre teaching, the increase in contingent faculty, and the use of online technology at the expense of a live teacher. Perhaps not surprisingly, these and other like-minded criticisms of the quality of undergraduate teaching and learning find some empirical support in a recent book by Richard Arum and Josipa Roksa entitled *Academically Adrift* (2010). Based on a study of some 2,300 undergraduates at 24 universities that focused on student studying and learning, Arum and Roksa found that students devote an average of little more than 12 hours per week to studying and that more than one-third of college and university seniors are no more skilled at basic reasoning and writing than they were in their first semester of college.

In the context of this unsettling body of literature, this chapter explores the discourse on the purpose of a college education over the past four decades. The first three sections of the chapter examine the dominant discourse, which argues that the longstanding legacy of liberal learning as the centerpiece of a college education has been eclipsed. The second section explores contemporary ideas regarding the purpose of a college education. The third section suggests that there remains a conspicuous absence of a keystone purpose of a college education, much less a purpose that is shared across our colleges and universities. In writing this chapter we often recalled the words of

Mark Van Doren in his classic volume entitled *Liberal Education:* "The one intolerable thing in education is the absence of intellectual design" (1943, p. 10).

The Dominant Discourse: Eclipse of the Legacy of Liberal Education

The idea of a liberal education, beginning with the Greeks in the fifth century BC, runs like a chartreuse thread through the history of higher education. One of the most compelling of the many books on the idea of liberal education is Bruce Kimball's *Orators and Philosophers* (1986). As elaborated on by Kimball, as well as by other historians of higher learning (Lucas, 2006; Rudolph, 1962; Rudolph, 1977; Schmidt, 1957; Thelin, 2004; Thomas, 1962; Veysey, 1965), a liberal education in the United States, from the founding of Harvard College in 1636 until well into the twentieth century, served as the foundation on which our colleges and universities were built. Even with the rise of comprehensive universities in the late nineteenth and throughout the twentieth century, the notion of liberal education continued to find expression in the nearly universal adoption of general education requirements and, no less, in liberal arts colleges, which have been committed to maintaining fidelity to the concept of liberal education across all four years of baccalaureate-level education (Conrad & Wyer, 1980).

Notwithstanding this celebrated history, undergraduate education—liberal education writ large and general education in particular—has received an unprecedented outpouring of severe criticism in recent decades. Amid the cacophony of voices surrounding the "crisis" and "crises" (Birnbaum & Shushok, 2001; Smith, 2004) in baccalaureate-level education, the dominant theme has been the eclipse of this historic legacy of liberal education. This theme is anchored in two interlocking streams of thought. The first is that there has been an eye-catching erosion of a common body of general knowledge and culture, commonly labeled "general education," as the centerpiece of a college education. The second is the rise of the "practical arts" (both professional and occupational education) at the expense of liberal and general education. Each of these streams is elaborated on below.

Decanonization: The Erosion of a Core
of General Knowledge and Culture

In the mid-1970s a national study sponsored by the Carnegie Council on Policy Studies in Higher Education reported that between 1967 and 1974 general education requirements, as a percentage of undergraduate curricula, had dropped dramatically (Blackburn et al., 1976). Drawing in part on that study, the Carnegie Foundation for the Advancement of Teaching concluded: "General Education is a disaster area" (1977, p. 11).

Since then an outpouring of voices has lamented the erosion of a common body of knowledge and culture as the core of a college education. Among many others, Herbert London expressed deep concern about the prospects for liberal and general learning in our colleges and universities. He argued that, given intense competition for limited space, time, and resources, "a ballot to determine the complexion of the curriculum is very often simply a pork barrel bid," driven by faculty anxious to preserve jobs and bolster enrollments; in turn, the general education curriculum has less to do with a core body of knowledge than a series of courses put together through "academic backscratching" (1978, p. 1).

Beginning in the early 1980s, a plethora of reports and writings bemoaned the loss of liberal learning, especially the humanities and general education. Based on their assessment that internal support among faculty members for the humanities was eroding and that funding from external sources for higher education had decreased, the Commission on the Humanities concluded: "Liberal education and the humanities, their fates still linked, were willed to the periphery of undergraduate learning" (1980, p. 66). Since then, the narrative of the loss of Western civilization—especially the canon of the Great Books and the humanities—as the centerpiece of a college education has been echoed by many groups and individuals both within and outside the academy.

Drawing on the Study Group on the State of Learning in the Humanities in Higher Education that he had assembled, the chairman of the National Endowment for the Humanities, William Bennett, issued a widely read report entitled *To Reclaim a Legacy* (1984). The report argued passionately that our colleges and universities were no longer preserving fundamental humanistic knowledge and culture—as embedded in the grand Western tradition—which ought to be at the heart of a college education. As the report put it, "Many of our colleges and universities have lost a clear sense of the importance of the humanities and the purpose of education, allowing the thickness of their catalogs to substitute for vision and a philosophy of education. The humanities, particularly the study of Western civilization, have lost their central place in the undergraduate curriculum. At best, they are but one subject among many that that students might be exposed to before graduating. At worst, and too often, the humanities are virtually absent" (p. 1).

In the late 1980s, the Carnegie Foundation for the Advancement of Teaching conducted a study of undergraduate education. Headed by the former U.S. Commissioner of Education, Ernest Boyer, the Carnegie Foundation visited 30 public and private colleges and universities, both interviewing and surveying academic deans, faculty, undergraduates, and high school students and their parents. In arguing for a renewal of undergraduate education, Boyer observed that we "are left with doubts about the quality of today's general education movement. During campus visits we found curriculum tinkering rather than genuine reform. We found that narrowly focused courses in English, science, and history often were easily relabeled 'general education.' And protecting departmental turf often seemed more important than shaping a coherent general education program" (1987, p. 87).

Reflecting this pervasive sense of loss across the contemporary discourse, a 1989 survey funded by the National Endowment for the Humanities and conducted by the Gallup Organization indicated that roughly one-quarter of the nation's college seniors were unable to locate Columbus's voyage to America within the correct half-century. About the same percentage could not distinguish Churchill's words from Stalin's, or Karl Marx's thoughts from the ideas of the U.S. Constitution. More than 40 percent did not know when the Civil War occurred. Most could not identify the Magna Carta, the Missouri Compromise, or Reconstruction. Most could not link major works by Plato, Dante, Shakespeare, and Milton with their authors. To the majority of college seniors, Jane Austen's *Pride and Prejudice*, Dostoyevsky's *Crime and Punishment*, and Martin Luther King Jr.'s *Letter from the Birmingham Jail* were clearly unfamiliar (Cheney, 1989, p. 11).

At least through the mid-1980s, the decline of liberal and general education was attributed mostly to the rise of specialized study and the widespread introduction of "cafeteria style" (elective) general education courses. But beginning in the late 1980s, the "culture wars" emerged as yet another major threat to the tradition of liberal education. Under the broad umbrella of multiculturalism, there were highly public "academic disputes over which texts should be taught in the humanities . . . [and] over the competing claims of Western and non-Western culture" (Graff, 1992, p. 9). While various voices made claims for the importance of incorporating multiculturalism in general education (Sarchett, 1995), one of the most visible spokespersons was Henry Louis Gates Jr. In *Loose Canons* (1992), Gates argued that the world in which we live—a world divided by nationalism, racism, and sexism—requires that multiculturalism and cultural diversity be incorporated into undergraduate education. In *The Opening of the American Mind: Canons, Culture, and History* (1996), Lawrence Levine suggested that the incorporation of multiculturalism was but a reflection of ongoing change throughout the history of our colleges and universities, and a change to be celebrated rather than feared.

Notwithstanding such claims, the dominant discourse over the last several decades has been that the growing diversity in undergraduate education—multiculturalism—has often embodied hostility toward Western culture, the humanities, and the very concept of a core body of knowledge (Jacoby, 1994). In the *Disuniting of America*, Arthur Schlesinger Jr. wrote: " 'Multiculturalism' arises as a reaction against Anglo- or Eurocentrism; but at what point does it pass over into an ethnocentrism of its own? The very word, instead of referring as it should to all cultures, has come to refer only to non-Western, nonwhite cultures" (1991, p. 74). In *The Closing of the American Mind*, Allan Bloom (1987) bluntly stated that our colleges and universities are no longer providing students with the knowledge of the grand traditions of literature and philosophy—traditions that help to ensure that a college-educated person is a "whole person." In a similar vein, Dinesh D'Souza, in *Illiberal Education: The Politics of Race and Sex on Campus* (1991), attacked the rise of the multicultural curriculum, which has often included the elimination of basic courses in Western civilization and, from his perspective, the loss of the historic identity of general education. And in *The Battle of the Books in Higher Education*, William Casement—albeit along with suggesting that the traditional canon should incorporate a wider range of texts—took on multiculturalists in no uncertain terms: "Anticanonists tends to see plurality when they should see unity, and vice versa. Their denial of universal truths not only falters on its own logic and nearsightedness, but it undercuts the validity of the political agenda it has been allied with" (1996, p. xi).

Especially over the past two decades, an outpouring of writings have addressed concern about the loss of a sense of the historic purpose of a college education, namely, to provide graduates with a common body of knowledge and culture, especially classical knowledge of Western civilization and the "Great Books." Reflecting on the widespread lack of agreement on the purpose and meaning of a general education in our colleges and universities, William Schaefer, in *Education without Compromise,* referred to liberal education as "The Great Pretender in Today's Colleges and Universities" (1990, p. 18). In *Excellence without a Soul* (2006, p. 21), Harry Lewis argued that the undergraduate curriculum in the United States has become "aimless." And many other works have argued that there has been a decanonization of higher education, especially a diminution of the Western canon in general and the humanities in particular, and with it a loss of the historic legacy of general education. These works include Bill Readings' *The University in Ruins* (1996); Victor Davis Hanson, John Heath, and Bruce S. Thornton's *Bonfire of the Humanities* (2001); Bruce Wilshire's *The Moral Collapse of the University* (1990); and Frank Donoghue's *The Last Professors* (2008).

Building upon this body of rhetoric with an ironic twist, William Deresiewicz, a former professor of English at Yale University, wrote a provocative article entitled "The Disadvantages of an Elite Education" (2008). He argues that even an elite education has become "profoundly anti-intellectual" (p. 27) and that the "system forgot to teach them [students] along the way to the prestige admissions and the lucrative jobs, that the most important achievements can't be measured by a letter or a number or a name" (p. 28).

Prominence of the Practical Arts to the Detriment of Liberal Education

Consonant with the dominant perspective that a fixed body of knowledge and culture, especially knowledge of Western civilization, is no longer at the forefront of college education, has been the rise of the practical arts: professional and occupational education. This rise, which includes vocational and technical education, has been fueled by numerous factors: public skepticism over the worth of liberal and general education; student demand; expectations from industry, government, and the military; declines in the national economy; fragmentation of knowledge in concert with the balkanization of disciplines; and the rise of for-profit colleges (Oakley, 1992). These market-driven forces have unmistakably fueled the rise of the practical arts over the last several decades—especially, but not exclusively, as reflected in the rapid growth of major fields of study in professional, occupational, and vocational programs of study.

At the beginning of this century, Brint (2002) reported that, whereas professional and occupational fields accounted for 45 percent of bachelor's degrees in the 1960s, they accounted for roughly 60 percent of bachelor's degrees by the turn of the century—with hundreds of institutions awarding at least 80 percent of their degrees in these fields. When compared with traditional fields of study in the liberal arts, preprofessional, professional, occupational, and vocational programs have become far more popular. Designed to prepare students for jobs, among the fastest-growing undergraduate fields over the past several decades have been in business, education, engineering, health professions, computer and information systems, and public administration (Brint et al., 2005).

Significantly, liberal arts colleges now constitute only a modest percentage of our institutions of higher education (Hartley, 2003). And the rise of the practical arts over the last few decades has transpired not only in universities but also in liberal arts colleges. As several observers (Breneman, 1994; Delucchi, 1997) have noted, many small, independent colleges have drifted away from their founding purposes as liberal arts colleges in recent years.

Over the last several decades, scores of individuals have bemoaned the triumph of the practical arts at the expense of liberal education. Along with often blistering critiques of the quality of degree programs in the professions and occupations has been a more sustained criticism: the rise of the practical arts has undermined the integrity of undergraduate education by substituting vocational training for a liberal education. Echoing Thorstein Veblen's indictment in *The Higher Learning in America* (1918), which argued that a crude utilitarianism was being inflicted on undergraduate education, Benjamin Barber (1992) contended that by the early 1990s there were two prominent, and diametrically opposed, models of higher education: the vocational and the purist. The former mirrors the marketplace in its purposes and aims, including providing students with training for jobs; the latter is a sanctuary from society—the traditional ideal of liberal education, which, by definition, is nonpractical. While Barber did not explicitly embrace the monastic view of a college education—one in which an educated person is someone who pursues learning solely for its own sake—he clearly aligned himself with those bemoaning the rise of the practical arts.

The rise of the practical arts has also been criticized by William D. Schaefer, who argued that our colleges and universities have "mindlessly mixed vocational and academic courses without continuity or coherence or anything approaching a consensus as to what really should constitute an education . . . . I believe that we should be . . . deeply concerned about this confusion of purpose—a confusion that has led colleges and universities to make fraudulent claims about their goals and missions as they package a hodgepodge of unrelated courses and incoherent requirements" (1990, p. xii).

Adding their perspective to the discourse, David Stewart and Henry Spille (1988) criticized institutions—particularly those institutions (with addresses ranging from shopping malls to post office boxes) that offer mostly professional and vocational programs—that, from their vantage point, granted academically suspect or even fraudulent degrees in professional and occupational fields. And in his book exploring the consequences of the Internet on higher education, David Noble (2001) disparaged the rhetorical claims regarding the putative benefits of online universities, arguing that they are little more than "digital diploma mills" offering problematic degrees in professional and occupational fields.

The Eclipse of Liberal Education

Due to the growing prominence of the practical arts, and notwithstanding the legacy of liberal education and general education as well as those liberal arts colleges that remain tethered to that legacy, there is a broad consensus across the higher learning community that there has been a loss of the historic definition of a liberal education, namely, an education that is grounded in the acquisition of a broad base of knowledge and culture in the Western canon and traditional fields of specialized study associated with the liberal arts, from the humanities and the arts to the social sciences and the sciences.[1]

Several years ago, Anthony Kronman, a former dean of the Yale Law School, wrote *Education's End: Why Our Colleges and Universities Have Given Up on the Meaning of Life*. Kronman described why he was disturbed about the loss of purpose in undergraduate education: "As I have watched the question of life's meaning lose its status as a subject of organized academic instruction and seen it pushed to the margins of professional respectability in the humanities . . . I have felt what I can only describe as a sense of personal loss on account of my very substantial investment in the belief that the question is one that can and must be taught in our schools" (2007, p. 7). Harry Lewis put it this way in *Excellence without a Soul:* "Universities have lost the sense that their educational mission is to transform teenagers, whose lives have been structured by their families and their high schools, into adults with the learning and wisdom to take responsibility for their own lives and for civil society" (2006, p. xiv).[2]

Contemporary Ideas on the Purpose of
a College Education

Throughout the twentieth century and early in this century, scores of ideas have been advanced regarding the purpose and meaning of a college education, including liberal education and general education. These include well-known writings from Daniel Bell (1966), Robert Maynard Hutchins (1936), Earl McGrath (1976), Mark Van Doren (1943), and Henry Wriston (1937), as well as such well-known publications as the 1945 Harvard Committee report *General Education in a Free Society*. More recent writings in this genre include Blanshard (1973), the Carnegie Foundation for the Advancement of Teaching (1978), Conrad & Johnson (2008), Gaff (1983), Kaplan (1980), Kimball (1986), Martin (1982), Martin (1994), Mulcahy (2008), Nussbaum (1997), and Wegner (1978). Along with these publications, institutions of higher learning and national higher education organizations have advanced various ideas regarding the purpose of a college education. In exploring these ideas, we organize this section around the rubrics "liberal education and general education," the "humanities," and "undergraduate education."

In concert with tracing the common ground in the evolution of the idea of a liberal education, D. G. Mulcahy recently argued that we need to reconsider the ideal of what it means to be an educated person. In his words:

Inspired by varying conceptions of a liberal education, the ideal of the educated person has come to mean a person of intellectual formation, one who possesses knowledge in depth and breadth, one who possesses the knowledge and skills of citizenship, and who is respectful of others and caring toward them, and one who is enabled to engage in thoughtful action. Bearing this in mind, the position adopted here is that the idea of the educated person needs to be recast in a way that retains its emphasis on what Newman called cultivation of the intellect, recognizes the importance of practical knowledge and education for action, accommodates the view that education of the whole person brings into play emotional, moral, and spiritual formation, and adopts a pedagogical stance that gives full recognition to the experience, capacities, and interests of the individual. (2009, p. 484)

Anchored in their observation that classical definitions of "liberal education had lost their meaning" (1984, p. xiv), Zelda Gamson, a professor at the University of Michigan, and other participants in a study of undergraduate education proposed that liberal education be reformulated as "liberating education." They defined a liberating education as comprising three main components: "First, it leads students to a broad critical awareness. Second, it helps them apply what they learn to everyday life. Third, it increases their sense of power" (p. xiv). Adding to the discourse, William Cronon (1998), a professor at the University of Wisconsin–Madison, identified 10 qualities of liberally educated individuals: "1) they listen and they hear, 2) they read and they understand, 3) they can talk with anyone, 4) they can write clearly and persuasively and movingly, 5) they can solve a variety of puzzles and problems, 6) they respect rigor not so much for its own sake but as a way of seeking truth, 7) they practice humility, tolerance, and self-criticism, 8) they understand how to get things done in the world, 9) they nurture and empower the people around them, and 10) they follow E. M. Forster's injunction from *Howard's End:* 'Only connect . . .'" (pp. 76–78).

Bartlett Giamatti, who at the time was the president of Yale University, advanced a definition of a liberal education that reflects much of the soaring rhetoric on the subject.

I believe a liberal education is an education in the root meaning of *liberal—liber,* "free"—the liberty of the mind free to explore itself, draw itself out, to connect with other minds and spirits in the quest for truth. Its goal is to train the whole person to be at once intellectually discerning and humanly flexible, tough-minded and open-hearted, to be responsive to the new and responsible for values that make us civilized. It is to teach us to meet what is new and different with reasoned judgment and humanity. A liberal education is an education for freedom, the freedom to assert the liberty of the mind to make itself new for the other minds it cherishes. (1988, pp. 109–10)

In recent years, many colleges and universities also have advanced statements of the purpose of a college education, which include both liberal and general education. To illustrate, in 2007 Harvard University Faculty of Arts and Sciences issued the *Report of the Task Force on General Education,* which identified four goals for the general education curriculum:

1. General education prepares students for civic engagement.
2. General education teaches students to understand themselves as products of—and participants in—traditions of art, ideas, and values.
3. General education prepares students to respond critically and constructively to change.
4. General education develops students' understandings of the ethical dimensions of what they say and do. (pp. 5–6)

Not surprisingly, numerous professors in the humanities have expressed ideas on the purpose of a college education that have placed the study of the humanities more or less at the core of a college education. An illustration of the rhetoric widely used by professors in the humanities is Robert Proctor's argument in *Education's Great Amnesia: Reconsidering the Humanities from Petrarch to Freud:*

> The humanities can . . . help to give continuity and coherence to our increasingly fragmented liberal arts curriculum in three general ways. They can help us choose a goal for liberal education which addresses our highest needs; they can offer a perspective on Western history; and they can show us how to use this perspective to understand and evaluate our own times. . . . [The history of the humanities] raises a series of questions concerning our past, present, and future which every graduate of a liberal arts college should be able to answer. (1988, p. 175)

For Proctor, these questions are:

1. What is the Greek and Roman concept of the human? How did the Greeks and the Romans understand the relationship of the individual human being to nature, society, and to that which transcends the human?

2. How and why did the Renaissance humanists transform the classical concept of the human?

3. What are the humanities? Why did they begin in the Renaissance? Why has the tradition of the humanities deteriorated in our own time?

4. What understanding of the self, of nature, and of society underlay the scientific revolution of the seventeenth century and the Enlightenment of the eighteenth century?

5. What problems concerning the Renaissance/modern understanding of the self and nature did Kant and Hegel attempt to solve? What have been the consequences of their attempts for modern thought?

6. When and how did the social sciences come into being? As moral theories, what do the social sciences say about the nature of the self, and the meaning and purpose of human existence?

7. What are the differences between ancient and modern moral philosophy? How can one attain wisdom and virtue today?

(1988, p. 175)

In *Cultivating Humanity: A Classical Defense of Reform in Liberal Education*, Martha Nussbaum, a professor at the University of Chicago, advanced a definition of a liberal education that focuses on the humanities.

The idea of 'liberal education'—a higher education that is a cultivation of the whole human being for the functions of citizenship and life generally—has been taken up most fully in the United States. . . . What does the 'cultivation of humanity' require? . . . Three capacities, above all, are essential to the cultivation of humanity in today's world. First is the capacity for critical examination of oneself and one's traditions—for living what, following Socrates, we may call the 'examined life. . . . [Second], Citizens who cultivate their humanity need, further, an ability to see themselves not simply as citizens of some local region or group but also, and above all, as human beings bound to all other human beings by ties of recognition and concern. . . . But citizens cannot think well on the basis of factual knowledge alone. The third ability of the citizen, closely related to the first two, can be called the narrative imagination. This means the ability to think what it might be like to be in the shoes of a person different from oneself, to be an intelligent reader of that person's story, and to understand the emotions and wishes and desires that someone so placed might have. (1997, pp. 9–11)

Lynne Cheney, during her tenure as Chairman of the National Endowment for the Humanities, wrote a monograph entitled *50 Hours: A Core Curriculum for College Students.*[3] After expressing deep concern about the fragmented state of undergraduate education in general and the humanities in particular—including the decline of requirements in courses in the history of Western civilization, history, and American or English literature—she proposed an "imagined core of studies" of 50 hours anchored in four domains of knowledge: cultures and civilizations, foreign language, concepts of mathematics, foundations of the natural sciences, as well as the social sciences and the modern world.

Standing alongside the writings on liberal and general education and the humanities, there have been numerous writings on the purpose of an undergraduate education, including what it means to be an "educated person." To illustrate, Henry Rosovsky, dean of the Faculty of Arts and Sciences at Harvard College, proposed this vision of an "educated person":

1. An educated person must be able to think and write clearly and effectively.

2. An educated person should have achieved depth in some field of knowledge. Cumulative learning is an effective way to develop a student's powers of reasoning and analysis, and for undergraduates this is the main role of concentrations.

3. An educated person should have a critical appreciation of the ways in which we gain and apply Knowledge and understanding of the universe, of society, and of ourselves. Specifically, he or she should have an informed acquaintance with the aesthetic and intellectual experience of literature and the arts; with history as a mode of understanding present problems and the processes of human affairs; with the concepts and analytic techniques of

modern social science; and with the physical and biological sciences.

4. An educated person is expected to have some understanding of, and experience in thinking about, moral and ethical problems. It may well be that the most significant quality in educated persons is informed judgment which enables them to make discriminating moral choices.

5. Finally, an educated American . . . cannot be provincial in the sense of being ignorant of other cultures and other times. It is no longer possible to conduct our lives without reference to the wider world in which we live. A crucial difference between the educated and the uneducated is the extent to which one's life experience is viewed in wider contexts. (*The Great Core Curriculum Debate,* 1979, pp. 7–8)

Derek Bok, while president of Harvard University, emphasized the importance of establishing common goals of an undergraduate education. In his book *Higher Learning,* Bok illustrated such goals in referring to the aims that Alverno College established for its students:

1. Develop effective communications skills.
2. Improve analytic abilities.
3. Strengthen problem-solving capacities.
4. Develop the ability to make value judgments.
5. Improve facility in social interaction.
6. Achieve understanding of the relationship between individual and environment.
7. Develop awareness and understanding of the contemporary world.
8. Develop understanding of and sensitivity toward the arts and a knowledge of the humanities. (Bok, 1996, p. 60).

More recently, Bok named eight wide-ranging purposes of an undergraduate education in his book *Our Underachieving Colleges:* "the ability to communicate," "critical thinking," "moral reasoning," "preparing citizens," "living with diversity," "living in a more global society," "a breadth of interests," "preparing for work" (2006, pp. 67–81).

In 2005, a major higher education association, the Association of American Colleges and Universities, advanced a vision of an undergraduate education, based on a dialogue with hundreds of colleges and universities about goals for undergraduate education, which has been adapted by scores of institutions throughout the country. In its 10-year campaign, "Liberal Education and America's Promise: Excellence for Everyone as a Nation Goes to College," the LEAP vision identifies the following learning outcomes as essential for success in today's world:

— *Knowledge of Human Cultures and the Natural and Physical World*
   Grounded in study of the sciences and mathematics, social sciences, humanities, histories, languages, and the arts
— *Intellectual and Practical Skills*
   Inquiry, critical and creative thinking
   Written and oral communication
   Quantitative literacy
   Information literacy
   Teamwork and problem-solving
— *Individual and Social Responsibilities*
   Civic knowledge and engagement—local and global
   Intercultural knowledge and competence
   Ethical reasoning and action
   Foundations and skills for lifelong learning
— *Integrative Learning*
   Synthesis and advanced accomplishment across general and specialized studies (Association of American College and Universities, 2007, p. 3)

In *The Marketplace of Ideas* Louis Menand argued passionately that the time to reexamine the century-old belief that a liberal arts education should be separate from utilitarian concerns is long past due. Yet while ostensibly resisting the purity of the liberal arts model and contesting the notion that the "practical is the enemy of the true," the heart of his argument was that the humanities need to be rescued as a central component of a liberal education. Ironically, Menand ended up celebrating the humanities, in general, and the liberal arts and sciences, in particular, as the heart of an undergraduate education. In his words: "What are the liberal arts and sciences? They are simply fields in which knowledge is pursued disinterestedly—that is, without regard to political, economic, or practical benefit" (2010, p. 55).

The Absence of a Fundamental Purpose of a College Education

Notwithstanding the advancement of various ideas in the contemporary discourse, for several reasons we suggest that thus far no purpose that captures the essence of a college education, extends across our nation's colleges and universities, and accommodates mission variation across our institutions of higher learning has emerged.[4] Drawing on John Henry Cardinal Newman's observation that "abstract statements are always unsatisfactory" (Svaglic, 1982, p. xviii), we suggest that the ideas that have been advanced consist mostly of well-intended but high-flying rhetoric, which fails to capture a compelling and overarching purpose that can inform the development of undergraduate curriculum—from program requirements to our teaching and learning and our assessment of student learning.[5] A representative example of the soaring rhetoric on the purpose of undergraduate education is the "Statement on Liberal Learning" advanced by the Association of American Colleges and Universities.

> A truly liberal education is one that prepares us to live responsible, productive, and creative lives in a dramatically changing world. It is an education that fosters a well-grounded intellectual resilience, a disposition toward lifelong learning, and an acceptance of responsibility for the ethical consequences of our ideas and actions. Liberal education requires that we understand the foundations of knowledge and inquiry about nature, culture and society; that we master core skills of perception, analysis, and expression; that we cultivate a respect for truth; that we recognize the importance of historical and cultural context; and that we explore connections among formal learn-

ing, citizenship, and service to our communities. We experience the benefits of liberal learning by pursuing intellectual work that is honest, challenging, and significant and by preparing ourselves to use knowledge and power in responsible ways. Liberal learning is not confined to particular fields of study. What matters in liberal education is substantial content, rigorous methodology, and an active engagement with the societal, ethical, and practical implications of our learning. The spirit and value of liberal learning are equally relevant to all forms of higher education and to all students. Because liberal learning aims to free us from the constraints of ignorance, sectarianism, and myopia, it prizes curiosity and seeks to expand the boundaries of human knowledge. By its nature, therefore, liberal learning is global and pluralistic. It embraces the diversity of ideas and experiences that characterize the social, natural, and intellectual world. To acknowledge such diversity in all its forms is both an intellectual commitment and a social responsibility, for nothing less will equip us to understand our world and to pursue fruitful lives. The ability to think, to learn, and to express oneself both rigorously and creatively, the capacity to understand ideas and issues in context, the commitment to live in society, and the yearning for truth are fundamental features of our humanity. In centering education upon these qualities, liberal learning is society's best investment in our shared future. (Association of American Colleges and Universities, 1998)

Notwithstanding occasional references, much of the contemporary discourse seems more or less oblivious to the rapidly changing, global, and uncertain world of the twenty-first century that is explored in the next chapter.[6] Indeed, many writings draw on arguments almost exclusively from the past, with little reference to the world in which college graduates will live and work (Wagner, 2008). To wit, in drawing on the legacy of a "liberal arts education" in *Cultural Literacy,* E. D. Hirsch Jr. (1987) argued that the animating purpose of an education should be a "common heritage" that is rooted in a literary canon of highly valued works drawn largely from the West. In a similar vein, Allan Bloom (1987), in *The Closing of the American Mind*

(1987), argued that our colleges and universities should provide students with a canon anchored in philosophy and literature that makes them aware of the (mostly Western) world and man's place within it. Finally, the rhetoric on the purpose of an undergraduate education continues to be dominated by fragmented points that are anchored in often unswerving allegiance to dualisms, which serve only to highlight our collective failure to advance a compelling definition and shared understanding of what it means to be a college-educated person. From our perspective, these dualisms—intellectual mastery versus personal development, breadth of knowledge versus depth of knowledge, knowledge versus skills, canonical knowledge versus character development, affective versus cognitive, professional/vocational versus liberal, science versus the humanities—all militate against a robust and inclusive definition of a college education.[7] Tethered loosely to these more or less hallowed dualisms, and their accompanying either/or discourse, the historically prevailing terms *liberal education* and *general education* have become little more than hollow phrases.

In light of the limitations of the contemporary discourse, we conclude that there remains a conspicuous absence of a unifying purpose of a college education in the twenty-first century—a purpose that encompasses the whole of the higher learning while also allowing for mission differentiation. As Allan Bloom stated more than two decades ago, "The university now offers no distinctive visage to the young person. He finds a democracy of the disciplines—which are there either because they are autochthonous or because there are no recognized rules for citizenship and no legitimate titles to rule. In short, there is no vision, nor is there a set of competing visions, of what an educated human being is. The question has disappeared, for to pose it would be a threat to peace" (1987, p. 337).

part two

Approaching Obsolete

Higher Learning in the Twenty-First Century

chapter two

A Rapidly Changing World
and the Need for a Response

Only a decade into the twenty-first century, higher education stands like a diver at the edge of a platform: toes tentatively curled over the edge, limbs carefully considering the long dive down and into the swirling waters of economic and societal change below. But unlike a diver, higher education appears not quite willing to take the plunge, even if it is necessary.

After all, we in higher education are not divers for the most part. We have chosen a calling that requires us to be thoughtful scholars and teachers. We study human nature; fastidiously research the laws of science; playfully investigate the patterns of mathematics; and we are artisans, shaping words into meaningful expression so that we may infuse the intellectual commons with new knowledge. And perhaps most significantly, we guide our students, encouraging them to embrace a passion for learning so that they, in turn, may fulfill their human potential.

At the present time, seismic change on a global scale is well under way, and higher education is no longer afforded the luxury of pure scholarship, teaching, and learning. Although myriad factors underlie this global change—political instability, war and terrorism, population growth, heightened demands for water and energy, environmental damage—the primary catalysts for the changes affecting higher education in the United States are market forces driven by a dynamically shifting economy, which demand the transfer of knowledge and innovation from our nation's universities to the marketplace.

Because of these demands, higher education's long dive, from the platform into the swirling streams of change below, is merely an illusion. In reality, the waters of change have risen to meet us, hastily ascending the platform, lapping at our feet, relentlessly demanding attention. Seemingly unabated, change streams through the doors of our institutions, flooding our scientific and medical research centers; driving student enrollment from the humanities and into professional schools; running amok with advertisements from for-profit universities; leading students and their parents astray with external rankings; and demanding economic life-saving devices, which almost always bear labels modified by the nearly ubiquitous terms *knowledge* and *innovation.*

These waters of change are powerful. Left unchecked, they will fundamentally reshape the role of higher education in our society, increasingly shifting it away from public service and toward service with economic incentives. During the current era, therefore, unless higher education takes measured steps to protect its vital center, it will become ever more market-centric in its focus and actions, which will not only diminish its contribution to the public good but also fundamentally reshape its role within society.

Nested within this context of fundamental change wrought by powerful economic incentives, college and university administrators, faculty, students, and external stakeholders lack a guiding vision that holds the promise of informing undergraduate education—from curriculum requirements and course design to teaching practices, and above all the learning experiences of our students. Indeed, one of the most formidable challenges ahead for higher education is the essential need to advance a vision of higher learning that revitalizes the meaning of a college-educated person for the twenty-first century in ways that help to ensure that our colleges graduates are prepared not only for the workplace but also to fulfill their human potential.

In this chapter we explore the world of the twenty-first century within which higher education is situated. We begin by advancing the proposition that higher education is increasingly being shaped by two market forces. The first demands human development from higher education in the form of student workforce preparation. The second is an increased demand for the knowledge and innovation that is created by university scholars and can be turned into marketable products and services, which are sold for profit within the global economy. The chapter then goes on to explore four external trends affecting higher education, all of which are powerful enough to fundamentally reshape both the role and the purpose of higher education in the United States. In so doing, we suggest that higher education must proactively shape the trajectory of these trends, lest it fall victim to the unpredictable effects of dynamic change and economic incentives, as has happened to four other vital sectors of our society—health care, the media, farming, and the mortgage industry. We conclude the chapter by suggesting that our colleges and universities need to strategically engage these external forces not only to ensure that college graduates are prepared for the dynamic world of the twenty-first century but also to preserve higher education's longstanding role in serving the public good.

The Rapidly Shifting U.S. Economy: From Industrial Production to Knowledge and Innovation

The U.S. economy is rapidly shifting away from a national economy driven by industrial production to a global economy driven by knowledge and innovation. These two economic drivers are easily distinguished from each other. In an industrial production economy, market value is generated by physical products manufactured through human labor. By contrast, in a knowledge and innovation economy, value is generated through the commodification of human intellect— the thoughts and ideas created by humans—which are, in turn, modified and inserted into the global marketplace as a commodity for sale.

Evidence of this dynamic shift in the economy is reflected in data from the United States Bureau of Labor Statistics. For the time period between 1992 and 2005, the bureau projected that the total share of manufacturing jobs would decline by 2005, accounting for one of every seven, or 14.3 percent, of all jobs in the country (U.S. Bureau of Labor Statistics, 2001). The bureau projects that manufacturing will continue its steady decline between 2008 and 2018, and that by 2018 the manufacturing sector of the economy will account for just 12.9

percent of total jobs—down from 17.3 percent in 1998 and 14.2 percent in 2008 (ibid., 2009). Conversely, two major occupational groups, service and professional, will supply more than one-half of the total employment growth during the 2008–18 period, and all but three of the top 30 fastest-growing detailed occupations will be found in professional and related occupations and service occupations. More specifically, service-related industries are expected to add 14.6 million jobs, and two professional employment sectors are expected to have significant employment growth: (1) business services, which are projected to add 4.2 million jobs; and (2) health care and social assistance, which are projected to add 4.0 million jobs (ibid.).

Significantly, this dynamic shift in the U.S. economy is global in scope and mercurial in speed, and it first achieved widespread public attention with the publication of Thomas Friedman's *The World Is Flat: A Brief History of the Twenty-first Century*. Friedman's analysis of global economic change, which has been labeled "globalization," extends beyond the worldwide disbursement of goods and services to the very nature of the social contract between governments and their citizens:

> "Globalization is the word we came up with to describe the changing relationships between governments and big businesses," said David Rothkopf, a former senior Department of Commerce official in the Clinton administration and now a private strategic consultant. "But what is going on today is a much broader, much more profound phenomenon." It is not simply about how governments, businesses, and people communicate, not just about how organizations interact, but is about the emergence of completely new social, political, and business models. "It is about things that impact some of the deepest, most ingrained aspects of society right down to the nature of the social contract," added Rothkopf. (2007, p. 48)

Friedman augmented this analysis by stating:

> I am convinced that the flattening of the world, if it continues, will be seen in time as one of those fundamental shifts or inflection points, like Gutenberg's invention of the printing press, the rise of the nation-

state, or the Industrial Revolution—each of which, in its day . . . produced changes in the role of individuals, the role and form of governments, the ways business was done and wars were fought, the role of women, the forms religion and art took, and the way science and research were conducted, not to mention the political labels that we as a civilization have assigned to ourselves and to our enemies. (p. 49)

As a result of his continuing research on developments within the global economy, Friedman (2011) has recently begun to target higher education as a key component in America's economic success in the global marketplace. Friedman argues that colleges and universities must focus upon training students to create new and innovative ideas because once students enter the workforce they will have to "find their extra" in order to compete. For in our hyper-connected global economy, American workers easily can be replaced by computers, robots, or foreign workers. But if, according to Friedman, higher education educates students to unlock, unleash, discover, and expand their ability to create new ideas, then they will be prepared for the workplace and their ability to remain gainfully employed will be better protected.

Friedman's observations call attention to the ongoing shift in the role of higher education in the United States. As a result of globalization, the U.S. economy is moving away from its manufacturing base and toward an emerging knowledge economy, and because universities are a primary source of knowledge in this country, higher education now plays an integral role in economic growth. Thus, American society has issued a siren call to its higher education institutions, and this call demands two vital services: the development of human capital and marketable knowledge and innovation.

The First Siren Call: Human Development

In the global knowledge and innovation economy, increasing numbers of American employers are demanding high levels of knowledge and skill from their employees, who must be capable of creating new knowledge and innovative ideas (Slaughter & Rhoades, 2004). Many of these employees are people who previously would have gone directly from high school into the workforce to learn manufacturing skills on the job. In order to capably create marketable knowledge and innovation, as distinguished from laboring to manufacture durable goods, potential employees must develop their intellectual capacity and cognitive skills by learning from accomplished experts, and in the United States, these experts are employed by universities, where they teach courses, advise students, and confer degrees. Accordingly, increasing numbers of employers and students look to colleges and universities for the competencies they need to secure desirable employees or gainful employment.

As a result, the desire to gain access to higher education has become nearly universal in the United States, and a college degree has in many ways become what a high school diploma became a century ago: the entry card for a self-supporting career and to knowledgeable citizenship (Ramaley, Leskes & Associates, 2002). Consider the following excerpt from the *Greater Expectations National Panel Report* of the Association of American Colleges and Universities:

> College attendance has grown so rapidly over the past four decades that now 75 percent of high school graduates get some postsecondary education within two years of receiving their diplomas. . . . Many students and parents see college primarily as the springboard to employment; they want job-related courses. Policy makers view college as a spur to regional economic growth, and they urge highly targeted workforce development. Business leaders seek graduates who can think analytically, communicate effectively, and solve problems in collaboration with diverse colleagues, clients, or customers. (Ramaley, Leskes & Associates, 2002, pp. 1–2)

Indeed, recent data demonstrate that enrollment in postsecondary degree-granting institutions grew from about 7 million in the mid-1960s to more than 15 million in 2001–2; moreover, this trend is expected to continue at about 1.3% per annum, ultimately resulting in more than 20 million students enrolled in postsecondary institutions by 2020 (Tierney & Hentschke, 2007, p. 29).

This shift toward universal access to higher education for millions of U.S. citizens is transforming the role of higher education within

American society, as evinced by the stark prediction of E. Gordon Gee, president of the Ohio State University. Referring to the heavy industry that once dominated the American economy, Gee said: "The universities of the 21st century are going to be the smokestacks of the century. . . . The notion of the large, massive public university that can exist in isolated splendor is dead" (Welsh-Huggins, 2010). Smokestacks of the century or not, the universal call for human development is buffeting higher education. Left unchecked, it stands to transform the role of higher education in fundamental ways, ensuring that the defining purpose of a college education will be to train students to become "workplace commodities" rather than adequately preparing them to adapt to the rapidly changing workplace of the twenty-first century and, ultimately, to realize their human potential.

The Second Siren Call: Knowledge and Innovation

Accompanying the nearly universal demand for college enrollment has been a precipitous increase in demand from the marketplace for the knowledge and innovation created by scholars at our colleges and universities. Because scholars create new knowledge and innovation through their research and applied technologies, the intellectual property of these scholars, as supported by their universities, provides a substantial source of economic growth, activity, and wealth. The breadth and scope of these effects find expression in the following excerpt by the former provost of Columbia University, Jonathan R. Cole, who engagingly describes the marketing and commodification of university research in the daily lives of millions of world citizens. It is a long quote, but, in fact, length is the point.

> We use products derived from ideas generated at our great research universities countless times a day—whether we realize it or not.
>   For example, in the morning you may brush your teeth with an electric toothbrush, then stagger into the kitchen, open the refrigerator, and take out some orange juice. The toothbrush can vibrate thousands of times a minute, creating fluid dynamics that can dislodge bacteria and plaque much more efficiently than an old-fashioned toothbrush;

the refrigerator has a compressed gas circulating through its coils; and the orange juice has been preserved while being shipped from a distant location. All three are based on discoveries made in university research departments. Contemplating that night's dinner, you take some steaks out of the freezer and make sure you have the ingredients for a salad. Most likely, you are not thinking about the fact that the meat's fine quality is a result of artificial insemination and scientific breeding techniques, both the result of university work, or that the special tomatoes on your counter have been genetically modified. You put a nice bottle of California wine into the fridge to chill, with nary a thought of the heartier vines made possible by research conducted by university enologists, then turn on your favorite FM radio station, made possible through university inventions over in engineering, for a little background news.

The station gives you a weather update, based on knowledge originating in the meteorological wings of universities. Then there are news stories about an earthquake that measures 7.5 on the Richter scale, the number of hurricanes predicted for this year, and the latest public opinion poll on the upcoming election, all of which are based on information learned through university research. You swallow the antibiotic your doctor prescribed for you, and then, as your conscience gets the better of you, decide to go out jogging. You bring along some Gatorade (another university invention) so you won't get dehydrated. As you begin, you notice that your muscles are sore from your last run, and that reminds you to order some flowers for your elderly mother—her hip replacement surgery is tomorrow. On your way home you stop at the closest ATM machine for some cash, which, of course, uses another university discovery, and later, when you're driving to work, you flip on the GPS to navigate a construction detour. A few minutes later, back on route, you use your E-Z Pass to glide through the bridge toll booth—which uses laser technology, not to mention computers—paying a premium for driving into the city during peak hours (congestion pricing is also a university invention).

Whatever your job, you are very likely to continue using methods and devices that are the fruits of university research once you reach the office. As the manager of a hedge fund, for example, you would be using sophisticated mathematical programs to help make investment decisions, and the mathematics and investment algorithms, of course, would be based on advances made in universities. When you entered the office, you would turn on the computer to find out how the foreign markets were doing. In fact, all day long you would be using the computer and the Internet, which also began with university discoveries. If your advertising agency was using focus groups, it would be basing its work on university research, and when you took your lunch break, and the clerk at the local deli swiped your sandwich and soda over the bar-code scanner, you would again be encountering a university discovery. Enough. The list could go on and on, but the point is clear. As we march through our daily lives, all of us are continually enjoying the benefits of discoveries made at our great universities. (2010, pp. 193–95)

All of these real-world, marketable products—all commodified from intellectual property created by scholars at universities—are evidence of the siren call issued by both private and public sector leaders for university-created knowledge and innovation. In exchange for access to this wellspring for economic growth, these leaders seek to contractually engage universities and their scholars by offering monetary incentives to individual researchers and, on a larger scale, to universities as a whole. As a result, the market-driven interest in licensing and patenting university research has grown substantially over the past decade, and this growth curve is expected to continue at an exponential rate in the coming decade. In short, the knowledge and innovation economy has rendered new forms of monetary incentives for universities and their scholars that, from our perspective, already are fundamentally reshaping education, transforming it from its historic commitment to serving the public good to being far more market-centric and driven by the goal of producing revenue.

These siren calls underscore reality of the twenty-first century, and what we suggest amounts to a clear imperative for higher education. While our colleges and universities must educate individuals who will create the intellectual products that drive the future economy, these outside forces—in a very real sense—have taken the reigns and are directing growth and expansion into the service of immediate and short-term gains. Below we outline further trends affecting higher education in particular and then suggest a purpose of a college education.

Four Trends Affecting Higher Education, All Driven by Monetary Incentives

In addition to society's siren call to higher education for human development and university-created knowledge and innovation, four powerful market-centric trends are buffeting the academy, and they, too, threaten to fundamentally reshape higher education in ways that have been heretofore unheralded. These external trends are all grounded in economic incentives—either the loss of revenue or the potential to gain sizeable revenues. But unlike society's siren calls for human development and university-created knowledge and innovation, all four of these market-centric trends are surreptitious, quietly threatening to catch higher education unaware of the fundamental change that has been wrought until well after that change has occurred.

Proliferation of For-Profit Colleges and Universities

The first trend is driven by the heightened demand for human development within the knowledge and innovation economy. This demand has catalyzed a significant increase in the number of for-profit universities, especially those granting baccalaureate, master's, and doctoral degrees. The business purpose of for-profit higher education is to maximize profit, and thus, teaching and learning are managed as market-driven services, rather than as a public good that is focused upon human development (Slaughter & Rhoades, 2004). As a result, the for-profit industry represents a fundamental shift in basic assumptions about higher education—a departure in public policy from exclusive reliance on public and private nonprofit institutions to produce the broad benefits of postsecondary education for society at large (Tierney & Hentschke, 2007, p. 2).

In the past two decades, for-profit institutions have experienced a rapid rise in scope, scale, and reach. Presently, there are more than

1,400 for-profit colleges and universities (FPCUs) in the United States offering study in more than 200 occupational fields (U.S. Department of Education, 2010). Between 2000 and 2008, enrollment grew rapidly, nearly tripling, to 1.8 million, and by 2010 enrollment had reached nearly 2 million students. Due in large part to this dynamic growth, for-profit institutions are trending toward a consolidation among very large, publicly traded postsecondary corporations, and the value of their stock rose 460 percent over the period 2000–2003, compared to a 24 percent loss for the Standard and Poor's 500-stock index. By 2010, the for-profit educational providers were among the fastest-growing and best-performing business in the United States, boasting a $32.8 billion market capitalization (National Consumer Law Center Report, 2005, p. 11).

If there is a single descriptor of for-profit institutions in the modern era, it is profit maximization. Market-driven analyses drive decisions at all levels. Thus, decisions such as where to locate branch campuses are based upon the employability of graduates within the local job market, and, concurrently, only a highly focused, narrow set of programs—all tailored to the local job market—are offered at each branch campus. According to Tierney and Hentschke (2007), this education-to-work trajectory is intentionally shaped through course offerings and curricula, all of which are developed centrally and usually by teams consisting of representatives from three categories: administrators, local employers, and curriculum development experts. Moreover, because for-profit institutions seek to provide marketable curricula in efficient time formats in order to maximize profit, the role of faculty, and the individuals who populate this role, differs fundamentally from what is found at non-profit public and private universities. Many faculty are employed on a part-time basis, and whereas relevant work experience and successful employment are necessary for hiring, scholarly research typically has not been a condition of hire or success. Standardized course materials are the norm, and if faculty do not use the materials or achieve the predetermined objectives, they are not rehired (103). In this way, for-profit institutions develop a business plan as distinguished from an educational plan, with the risk built in—they assume little risk from the faculty because they do not think academic freedom, tenure, shared governance, research, and service facilitate profit maximization.

As a result of these varied mechanisms, the for-profit sector is redefining the meaning of higher education for millions of students across the country.[1] Tellingly, the success of for-profit institutions suggests that public universities and colleges are not only failing to inform the public of the major differences between for-profit and public institutions but also failing to meet the societal demand for human development.

Rapid Increase in Adjunct Faculty

The second trend affecting higher education is the rapid decline in the number of tenure track faculty at not-for-profit institutions. This phenomenon is driven by the goal of cutting expenses and is demarcated by a precipitous increase in the number of contingent employees, also known as adjunct faculty, who teach college courses. According to the American Association of University Professors, non-tenure-track positions now account for 68 percent of all faculty appointments in American higher education (American Association of University Professors, 2010). Because they are paid far less than tenure-track faculty, these contingent employees facilitate cost-savings for institutions of higher education. But at what price over the long term? Because contingent faculty can be terminated far more quickly and expeditiously than tenure-track faculty, they do not have the employment security to speak out freely and have little incentive to engage in research. In comparison to tenure-track faculty, contingent faculty are less likely to raise controversial issues; less likely to engage in research; and because they are likely to have another job elsewhere, they are less likely to have as much time as traditional faculty to address the needs of their students.

Academic Capitalism

With respect to the third trend, Slaughter and Rhoades (2007) have organized the economic activities related to commodifying university-created knowledge and innovation into marketable products under a useful label: *academic capitalism*. This umbrella term covers a pervasive trend in higher education: substantial monetary incentives from private industry have infiltrated the academy, shaping not only administrative decision-making and leadership priorities but also, and more significantly, shaping research and the pursuit of knowledge.

This trend comprises several powerful facets, the most powerful of which have unintended consequences resulting from the increased role played by universities in driving economic gain within the knowledge and innovation economy. Specifically, the volume and free flow of basic scientific research, as well as the new scientific knowledge it generates, is at risk because of the rapid increase in the number of contracts between private entities, universities, and individual researchers, most of which offer sizeable monetary incentives for university-created knowledge and innovation. In isolation, an increased number of contractual relationships between corporations, universities, and their scholars would not be detrimental; indeed, the corporate sector has long turned to colleges and universities for guidance and expertise.

There is a downside, though, to an increased volume of this activity. The more that university researchers engage in contractual relationships for purposes of generating technology transfer or testing existing corporate products prior to sale, the less basic scientific research is accomplished by these scientists. As a result, the free flow of basic research and the new scientific knowledge that it generates are at risk. In the future, this diminished wellspring of basic scientific research will, in turn, diminish the volume of applied technologies and technology transfer: where there is no basic scientific research, there can be no applied technology or technology transfer.

For example, once university researchers are under contract, they are captured by the industry that funds their contract—completing research on behalf of private companies, as distinguished from completing basic scientific research on behalf of their own research interests and the public good. And even though an individual researcher's contract-related work must be reported to the university as private research, which is often labeled an "outside activity," most scholars are free to enter into private contracts on an individual basis. Thus, these researchers may freely choose to refrain from studying basic scientific research questions—which would advance public knowledge and serve the public good but which may ultimately be unmarketable—seeking instead to earn additional income by pursuing lines of research tied to products supported by private industry through contractual engagements. In other words, these private contracts offer powerful monetary incentives, and most universities have no way of knowing whether a researcher has opted to contract with a corporation for applied research or market testing instead of choosing to pursue a line of basic research. Therefore, through the cumulative choices made by individual researchers at institutions of higher education across the country that allow private contracts, the wellspring of basic scientific research will surely decline in volume. This is particularly disconcerting because where there is diminished basic scientific research there will be diminished applied technology and technology transfer to drive future economic growth. Evidence of this phenomenon abounds.

The Chronicle of Higher Education has reported on the proliferating partnerships between universities and large pharmaceutical companies, such as Pfizer, AstraZeneca, and Gilead Sciences (Blumenstyk, 2011, pp. A1, A3–A4). Because these companies have cut back significantly, or even dismantled, their own research and development teams, they are actively engaging public and private universities by forming contractual partnerships through which universities, such as Vanderbilt, Yale, and the University of North Carolina at Chapel Hill, have all taken on the high-stakes work of drug discovery in exchange for millions of dollars in research support. In addition, these universities have hired former executives and researchers from pharmaceutical companies, evincing a revolving-door relationship between these companies and the universities they support financially.

Another powerful aspect of academic capitalism is that higher education institutions and their researchers are not only increasingly driven to secure monetary incentives from corporations, but many of these institutions also actively lobby state and federal legislatures to change regulations so that universities may expand their engagement in market and market-like behaviors. As a result, on an ever-increasing basis, faculty at public institutions are allowed to hold equity in private corporations founded upon their public research. While these private equity holdings are widely portrayed as a monetary incentive for professors to move technology to the marketplace, these holdings often create conflicts of interest that divide faculty loyalty between public universities and private businesses. Multiple unintended consequences result, including conflicts of interest, disputes regarding private ownership of public data, restricted or delayed publication of research findings, and a reduced volume of freely shared information within the intellectual commons.

Decline in Public Funding for Higher Education

The final trend affecting higher education in the twenty-first century is the consistent reduction in public funding for higher education. In part, this trend has been driven by difficult economic conditions, which have reduced state tax rolls and subsequently required government leaders to cut state budgets. Because public higher education spending is considered discretionary, as distinguished from mandatory spending on prisons or hospitals, and because higher education can recoup its loses through raising tuition rates, state leaders often turn to higher education when executing budget cuts.

Concurrent with reductions in public funding and the substantial increase in the volume of contracts and economic incentives proffered to universities and their scholars by private corporations, the warp-drive speed of change within the knowledge and innovation economy demands that higher education act quickly to gain monetary benefits. But by uncritically responding to these monetary incentives, higher education stands to lose, or at least unwittingly diminish, fundamental aspects of its core purpose within society. Inevitably, therefore, through the shift from public funding to ever-increasing private funding, service to the public good will diminish, having been supplanted to some extent by service to the goals and objectives of private funders.

Reduced public funding for higher education is also driven by the change in public perception of the value of a college degree. In prior decades, a college degree was perceived to be a public good—increasing the income tax rolls through the higher wages earned by college graduates; increasing the volume of community service; and increasing the volume of industries drawn to a region because of the number of college graduates residing there. At the present time, however, the public primarily perceives a college degree to be a private good—serving above all the individual who earns the degree and who possesses, therefore, the ability to earn a higher wage than someone without a college degree. Hence, the diminished support for higher education both in terms of tax dollars and public perception has resulted in higher tuition rates for students. Consequently, many students, and especially those of lower socioeconomic status, have difficulty affording the universities that have accepted them. In turn, society stands to lose the human potential that would have been actualized had these students from lower socioeconomic backgrounds been able to attend public colleges and universities.

Lessons from Other Sectors of Society, All Reshaped by the Same Market Forces Buffeting Higher Education

Many institutions of higher education simply do not have the framework necessary to manage the powerful market-centric forces at play in the twenty-first century. Accordingly, the rising tide of change driven by market forces may overwhelm much of higher education, flooding its banks and dictating its future. Consider the prediction issued at the turn of the twenty-first century by James Duderstadt:

> While most of our colleges and universities are changing to adapt to a changing world, they are not yet transforming themselves into educational institutions suitable for our future. The glacial pace of academic change simply may not be sufficiently responsive to allow the university to control its own destiny. There is a risk that the tidal wave of societal forces could sweep over the academy, both transforming higher education in unforeseen and unacceptable ways while creating new institutional forms to challenge both our experience and our concept of the university. (Duderstadt, 2000, p. 9)

Simply stated, unless higher education makes a concerted effort to proactively respond to the complex and powerful external forces at play, it will be reshaped by these market forces, which will transform higher education's role within society in fundamental and potentially inalterable ways, moving it away from service to the public good and toward service to market forces.

As higher education leaders reflect on the societal demands and market trends brought about by the shift to a knowledge economy, we find it instructive to reflect on the changes already being wrought by the powerful economic incentives fueled by the knowledge economy to four other fundamental sectors of society: health care, the media, family farms, and even the American Dream of home ownership. These four sectors of society—which were previously grounded in public service—have all become market centric, primarily grounded in profit-driven motives. These sectors provide important lessons for higher education, clearly indicating that stakeholders within higher education must take heed, carefully managing the powerful economic incentives that have risen to meet them.

Consider, for example, how publicly traded health maintenance organizations (HMOs) have inalterably revised the work of doctors, as well the collective experience of patients who encounter the medical profession. Not so long ago, doctors made house calls. Through relatively small partnerships, groups of physicians were often woven into their communities and able to provide care on a for-patient rather than a for-profit basis. The doctors were in charge, not the publicly traded HMOs. Moreover, hospitals were once independent, non-profit institutions, committed to serving the purpose of preserving and protecting human life as distinguished from serving shareholders and profit motives.

Consider further that reporting the news was once closely linked to preserving free speech in society and informing citizens as partners in a democratic form of government. Then consider how many reporters and news agencies have been subsumed within the entertainment industry, within for-profit media conglomerates. How can Americans make informed decisions within a democratic society when the goal of many media institutions is to maximize quarterly profits by entertaining and enticing as wide an audience as possible?

Consider, too, the exponential growth of factory farms, which have supplanted family farms at escalating rates and which are owned by publicly traded agribusinesses. Family farmers used to abound in rural communities, with the common goal of providing for both their families and their communities. But no more. In 2000 a total of four agribusinesses produced 81 percent of cows, 73 percent of sheep, 57 percent of pigs, and 50 percent of chickens annually consumed in the United States (*Congressional Record*, 2000, pp. 56–65). At factory farms, animals are confined at high stocking densities so as to raise and slaughter the highest possible number of animals at the lowest cost. As a result, untreated waste pollutes local environments and, because the animals are routinely fed antibiotics and antibacterial medications to ward off the diseases that result from close confinement, those of us who consume meat from these animals are more susceptible to bacteria that have developed a resistance to these same medications, which in turn renders it more difficult for us to ward off disease.

Finally, consider how the concept of home ownership has been commodified by publicly traded, national investment banks seeking to maximize profit and quarterly market gains. Owning a home used to be the pinnacle of the American Dream, proof positive of economic success. Home mortgages used to be primarily originated and held by local community banks, which carefully evaluated the financial stability of each homeowner prior to lending money. In recent years, home mortgages began to be sold in ever-increasing numbers by community banks to publicly traded, national investment banks. Unraveling the 2008 bailout of these banks by the U.S. government demonstrated that these banks recast the mortgages of millions of regular people's homes, transforming them into billions of dollars' worth of bonds and derivative financial instruments—all of which were unregulated by the federal government. As a result, many people were incentivized to no longer consider "home" as a place to raise their children, invest their savings, or rest at the end of a long day. Instead, "home" became a place to gain easy money through first and second mortgages, which were then grouped together by investment banks into billions of dollars of unregulated bonds that lost most of their value in 2008, when many people could no longer afford to pay mortgages they probably should never have taken out in the first place.

Proactively Directing External Forces and Preparing Students for a New World

Now is not the time for higher education to stick its proverbial head into the sand. As evinced by its collective effects upon other fundamental sectors of society—as well as the shift in the purpose, delivery, and public perception of higher education that is already well under way in the for-profit sector—the economic change that has risen rapidly to meet not only our institutions but also our students, faculty, and staff is far too powerful to ignore. The challenge is this: either stakeholders within higher education will shape the future of higher education, or higher education will be haplessly shaped by the external forces acting upon it. For the most part, these external forces are not animated by an ethos of service to the public good; instead, they are market driven—grounded in a desire to turn a profit in the global marketplace and led by individuals acting on their own behalf and on behalf of the companies and shareholders for whom they provide leadership.

Moreover, at this juncture in history, not only do universities stand at risk, but so too does society itself stand at risk. Crucially, therefore, higher education must provide guidance both within its own ranks and to a society that urgently needs its expertise in such domains as navigating change on a global scale, preserving strained global resources, responding to profound environmental damage, managing unheralded population growth, and riding out political and economic upheaval. There is much at stake.

But there also is hope. For if we carefully consider the lessons to be learned from the four other sectors of society that have undergone fundamental change—health care, the media, farming, and the mortgage industry—higher education stands in a vastly stronger position than each of them. Higher education holds the leverage to shape its own destiny because our colleges and universities have what society desperately needs—the ability to provide human development and the capacity to create knowledge and innovation needed for economic growth. In other words, because higher education is the wellspring of human development, as well as a primary source of the new knowledge and innovation that can drive economic wealth, it holds the power to set forth the rules of engagement that inform the human development we foster and to govern the release of our knowledge and innovation to those who seek to profit from our ingenuity, scholarship, and intellectual commons. In short, the power to direct the external forces that are buffeting higher education is well within reach.

As challenging as it will be to achieve this goal, the quest is not quixotic. First and foremost, we must ensure that our institutions of higher learning are centered upon serving the public good. To that end, the map for navigating the road ahead must be based on an overarching purpose of a college education that guards against higher education becoming little more than an assembly line primarily focused on delivering students who are turned out for the existing workplace. We must also capture a fundamental purpose of an undergraduate education that prepares college graduates for the rapidly changing world of the twenty-first century. In chapter 4 we set forth a purpose that represents a fundamental "re-booting" of higher learning. We believe that refocusing higher learning on preparing what we refer to as "inquiry-driven" learners will help to address the root challenges of the economic change at hand, which threatens to erode our current system of higher education. To begin with, individuals who embrace an ethos of inquiry are far better equipped than otherwise to parry the wiles of short-term capitalistic gains. For example, such individuals have the capacity to reshape society's current deployment of for-profit institutions into supplemental institutions that fill niche needs of society as a whole rather than the pockets and bank accounts of a few. Finally, those who embody the capabilities of an inquiry-driven learner are well-suited to communicate the value of education—inquiry in particular—to a public that is increasingly skeptical about committing shared and scarce resources with institutions that have been caught planning for the present rather than the future.

In summary, a clear and compelling purpose of a college education is needed to inform undergraduate education—the curriculum and course design, the extracurriculum, everyday teaching practices, and above all, the learning experiences of students—in ways that will enable college graduates to adapt to the dynamically changing world we live in and fulfill their human potential, as well as contribute to their communities, society, and humanity.

chapter three

Hurtling toward Obsolescence

The Default Purpose of a College Education

Ironically, at the same time that colleges and universities in the United States should be educating creative and disciplined problem-solvers who are prepared to navigate the unchartered and turbulent waters of the twenty-first century, most institutions have adopted a default purpose of a college education that remains more or less oblivious to the world we live in. In broad strokes, this default purpose is centered on providing students with foundational knowledge—both general and specialized—and ensuring that they have the skills needed for securing employment or pursuing postbaccalaureate study before joining the workforce.

In this chapter we argue that this default purpose of a college education fails because much of the knowledge and many of the skills acquired by students will not be relevant by the time the ink on their diplomas is dry. Put another way, an education that focuses primarily on the acquisition of knowledge and the skills relevant only for current jobs is not preparing students to adapt to the sweeping and constant change that has become a distinguishing feature of the global world that is emerging. As Joshua Ramo, in *The Age of the Unthinkable,* put it in his portrait of global change in the twenty-first century: "We are now at the start of what may become the most dramatic change in the international order in several centuries, the biggest shift since European nations were first shuffled into a sovereign order by the Peace of Westphalia in 1648. . . . As much as we may wish it, our world is not becoming more stable or easier to comprehend. We are entering, in short, a revolutionary age" (2010, pp. 7–8).

Just when our dynamically changing world calls for human development that far exceeds knowledge acquisition and workforce preparation, most of our colleges and universities seem focused primarily on providing students with a foundation of general and specialized knowledge and on preparing them for the contemporary workplace—not for a constantly changing workplace and for living well as individuals and citizens in the twenty-first century. We hardly stand alone in making such arguments. To take but one example, Martha Nussbaum has recently argued that many of our colleges and universities are not adequately preparing students for citizenship; in her words, we are not "cultivating humanity."

> Radical changes are occurring in what democratic societies teach the young, and these changes have not been well thought through. Thirsty for national profit, nations and their systems of education are heedlessly discarding skills that are needed to keep democracies alive. If this trend continues, all over the world we will soon be producing generations of useful machines, rather than complete citizens who can think for themselves, criticize tradition, and understand the significance of another person's sufferings and achievements. The future of the world's democracies hangs in the balance. (2010, p. 2)

In exploring the default purpose of a college education, we begin by critiquing its two fundamental components: knowledge-centrism and the education of workplace commodities. In turn, we argue that it is vitally important to guard against higher education becoming little more than an assembly line that is focused primarily on delivering knowledge and workplace credentials—both of which fall short of preparing students to lead fulfilling lives amid the dynamic change inherent in the unfolding century. The chapter closes with our call for a defining purpose of a college-educated person in the twenty-first century.

Shortcomings of the Default Purpose: Knowledge-Inundated, Workplace Commodities

From our perspective, there are two fundamental shortcomings in the default purpose. First, it emphasizes knowledge-stuffing: students are above all expected to acquire knowledge and information—facts, figures, equations, formulas, information—rather than developing what matters far more: the capacity to pursue promising and innovative ideas for a rapidly changing world. Second, the default purpose reifies a college education as a credential for entering the existing workforce rather than as a unique opportunity to cultivate capabilities that prepare students for the future. Below we elaborate on the two major components of the default purpose and their respective shortcomings.

Knowledge-Inundation

Many of us in higher education celebrate knowledge in our roles as custodians and producers of knowledge. As such, we wittingly or unwittingly place the delivery of knowledge and information at the center of a college education. While an emphasis on knowledge-acquisition is a defining feature of most specialized programs of study, the centrality of knowledge-imparting is nowhere more manifest than within general education, which has long remained an integral component of undergraduate education in the United States.

The evolution of general education in recent years can in no small measure be traced to *General Education in a Free Society: Report of the Harvard Committee.* This 1945 report set an agenda for general education requirements in the nation's secondary schools, in the higher education establishment, and in society at large. The authors of the report declared their purpose to be a "quest for a concept of general education that would have validity for the free society which we cherish," and they set forth a knowledge triumvirate consisting of the humanities, social studies, and science and mathematics. Ironically, while the Harvard Committee sought to rehabilitate these traditional categories from signifying "inert knowledge" to signifying "methods of knowledge" (p. 59), maintaining these three areas of knowledge in its conceptualization of general education has, over time, reinforced the conventional view of knowledge as defined in content-based terms.[1]

We suggest that the continuing and widespread emphasis in higher education on imparting content, whether the emphasis is on breadth or depth of knowledge, is not an optimal guiding principle for undergraduate education. Most important, making "knowledge-imparting"—both in general education and in areas of concentration—the centerpiece of a college education reinforces the conventional view that knowledge is something to be passively received rather than actively pursued. Such a perspective is not a new realization. Throughout the history of American higher education, there have been various efforts to recast the emphasis away from knowledge acquisition, as reflected in the "knowledge-imparting" instructional paradigm that has long informed undergraduate education. Take, for example, the following passage from the foreword to the National Educational Alliance's *The Popular Educator Library: A Liberal Education of University Standard* (1940): "Since in many respects it is a new departure in the science of teaching, it may be well to explain to the reader something of the plan and organization of the work. The real intent of our lectures is to make readers think. True education is not merely to stuff people's heads with facts: it consists in so instructing the studious reader that he becomes capable of using his own reasoning powers for his own further instruction" (p. v).

The 1828 Yale Report's emphasis on "discipline of the mind," and more recently, the innumerable calls for faculty to be "a guide on the side" rather than "a sage on the stage," set forth a simple message: higher education ought not give primacy to the mere transmission of knowledge (Barr & Tagg, 1995). Still, no matter how well some colleges and universities have endeavored to distance themselves rhetorically from a knowledge-imparting view of undergraduate education, most institutions continue to maintain de facto allegiance to such a view. This allegiance is reflected not only in general education programs but also in specialized fields of study—majors, minors, and concentrations. By so doing, most institutions employ the knowledge triumvirate reified in the Harvard Committee's "Redbook" of 1945, namely, the humanities, social studies, and science and mathematics. Thus, in their specialized fields of study as well as in their required general education courses, students are routinely expected by college and university faculty to focus on the acquisition of knowledge and information that is variously delivered via lecture, books, articles, and online blog postings and the like.

We suggest, then, that engaging students in honing their abilities to exercise independent thought, reasoning, and problem-solving receives far too little attention in our colleges and universities. As Sarah Lawrence-Lightfoot put it in her critique of contemporary education, "The goals of schooling tend to be shortsighted and narrowly pragmatic. We work to prepare our young people for the next step in the educational pyramid, or the first level of employment, and we ignore the long view. . . . Curiosity, risk-taking, questioning, experimentation are largely written out of classroom conversations. . . . [In short, educational] values and practices may distort organic learning across the life span, compromising and masking the impulses that might make us productive and creative learners when we are no longer living within the constraints of school or work environments" (2009, pp. 235–36).

To be sure, scores of promising innovations have been introduced in many colleges and universities—innovations often falling under the rubrics of "liberal education" and "general education"—that are aimed at equipping students with far more than a foundation of knowledge and preparation for employment in the existing workplace. Moreover, there are faculty across our colleges and universities who are passionately committed to advancing student learning, not only in general education courses but in specialized fields of study as well, in ways that extend far beyond knowledge acquisition and workforce preparation. Notwithstanding these innovations and faculty initiatives, we are persuaded that they are exceptions to the dominant narrative.

This message is critical in the modern era, for the twenty-first century is one of ceaseless change. And this change cannot be ignored. As Joshua Ramo puts it: "This change is irresistible. It is infectious. It will spread to every corner of our lives, to our businesses, our bank accounts, our hopes, and our health" (2010, p. 8). Without the ability to adapt to this constant change, our students are not being educated to navigate the world of the twenty-first century. In short, the widely embraced "knowledge-imparting" philosophy of undergraduate education leaves college graduates inadequately prepared to adapt to uncertain and rapidly changing local, regional, national, and global environments—all of which call for individuals who are able to address complex and often unanticipated challenges in their personal, public, and workplace lives. We cannot, as Ramo argues, face the future with "ideas, leaders, and institutions that are better suited for a world now several centuries behind us" (ibid.) In short, we must cultivate in our students the capacity to develop new ideas—not simply acquire and apply existing knowledge—if they are to be prepared to address the myriad challenges they must face in the tumultuous twenty-first century.

A twenty-first-century college education must also prepare students to reflect on the knowledge and ideas that are developed—including their own—in response to such pressing social issues as exploding population growth; the rising scarcity of natural resources, especially fresh water in certain regions of the world; the increasing cost, and finite supply, of fossil fuel energy; the increasing deterioration of the Earth's climate and ecology; and the instability of many world governments, including those that possess nuclear weaponry. Jeremy Rifkin argues that humanity will survive these complex, life-threatening challenges only if we humans learn to empathize with one another, appreciate the challenges faced by those outside our respective inner circles, and most importantly, take action to protect those other than ourselves. In his words,

> Nothing could be more important at this juncture in our history as a species than to have a meaningful cultural debate about the role empathy has played in the development and conduct of human affairs. Such a debate is no longer an esoteric exercise but, rather, a life-or-death imperative for our species. Our ever more complex energy-consuming global civilization is careening the human race to

the very brink of extinction. If our scientists are right, we may be within a century or so of our possible demise on this planet. . . . The task before the human race is daunting. For the first time, we have to defy our won history as a species and create a new, more interdependent civilization that consumes less rather than more energy, but in a way that allows empathy to continue to mature and global consciousness to expand until we have filled the Earth with our compassion and grace rather than our spent energy. (2010, pp. 177–78)

Along with implicitly questioning the centrality of knowledge-centrism in undergraduate education, Rifkin's arguments suggest that it is imperative for undergraduates to understand and appreciate that human interconnectedness is a hallmark of the world in which we all live, and therefore, they must pursue lines of inquiry that reflect their commitment to humanity and the public good.

Workplace Commodities

In addition to imparting knowledge, the default purpose of an undergraduate education holds forth that the primary purpose of higher education is to produce "commodities" for the workplace. As such, this default purpose is essentially representing an economic theory that places primary emphasis on the individual—objectified and reduced to an economic actor. By embracing this input-output model, the default purpose emphasizes the role of colleges and universities in preparing economic actors for the workplace who will, above all else, contribute to the economic well-being of the nation.

In emphasizing the development of the kinds of human capital demanded by the existing workplace, many colleges and universities focus mostly on short-term individual and societal economic needs. Indeed, it has become increasingly common to describe undergraduate education in terms of a business model. As characterized by Hersh and Merrow, business and industry communicate their needs and, in turn, educational institutions dutifully turn out students who can head straight to the factory floor or the office cubicle. Educational quality in this scheme is indicated by the market value of a degree—

often established by a ranking of a school or department or program—and the efficiency with which the respective institution is able to move a student to a degree that secures a good job. Significantly, a majority of undergraduate students seem to have embraced the claim that an undergraduate education is about commodity production and, in turn, that gainful employment is the end goal of an undergraduate education. As Hersh and Merrow (2005, pp. 6–7) put it: "They [students] accept, apparently unthinkingly, the existence of a one-to-one relationship between college and work, as if the entire purpose of going to college was to enable graduates to 'get a good job.' It is as if they somehow believe they will be working twenty-four hours a day." In short, many graduates are narrowly educated, with little preparation for life beyond securing jobs in the short-term workplace, because the "career education" bandwagon emphasizes the preparation of students to land high-paying jobs. And significantly, less and less attention is being placed on cultivating meaningful connections between higher education, the development of human potential, and the public good writ large.

As discussed in the previous chapter, workforce development is nowhere more explicit than within the for-profit sector of higher education. For-profits determine where to locate branch campuses based upon the employability of their graduates in the local job market, and they concomitantly offer a highly focused, narrow set of programs at each campus that are tailored to the local job market (Tierney & Hentschke, 2007).

While the nation's elite colleges and universities overtly separate themselves from the for-profits, many of these institutions also are focused on workforce preparation at the undergraduate level. Rather than preparing "workers," with standardized knowledge and skills, many prestigious institutions are preparing "workplace and societal leaders" along with providing membership dues for entry into the "upper class" of society. As William Deresiewicz (2008) argues, "elite schools speak of training leaders, not thinkers—holders of power, not its critics" (p. 29). He concludes, "Our best universities have forgotten that the reason they exist is to make minds, not careers" (p. 20).

From our perspective, this widespread emphasis on preparation for the immediate workplace is deeply flawed. To begin with, history is filled with examples of failed social experiments that treated people as work units rather than as individuals capable of inspiration and ingenuity (Nussbaum, 2010). Most important, in a world of rapid and constant change, a focus on preparing college graduates for an economy in which they may find short-term employment is wholly inadequate in the long run. Graduates must be prepared to adapt to constantly changing environments, as well as to participate in sustaining and reconstructing the environments in which they find themselves. A "workplace commodity" may be prepared for employment in the existing workplace, but our college graduates must be prepared for a rapidly changing workplace, in which they are likely to change jobs and even careers numerous times over the course of their lives.

In short, the never-ending change that has become the twenty-first century norm demands that higher education prepare students—as often expressed in everyday discourse—for jobs that do not yet exist. Because technology advances so rapidly, what we understand today as the workplace will be vastly different in the coming years, as technological advancements take hold, evolve, and reshape the workplace and the workforce. In turn, the workplace will rely far less on individuals with narrow technical or job-focused training and far more on people who have capabilities that will enable them to adapt to a fluid workplace.

The Need for a Fundamental Purpose of a College Education

Rather than hurtle toward obsolescence by genuflecting to the default purpose of a college education—developing knowledge-inundated, workplace commodities—we need colleges and universities that have articulated and maintain fidelity to an overarching purpose that will help prepare students for the future. Indeed, if we fail to set forth a purpose for a college-educated person and uncritically continue to pay homage to the default purpose, we risk betraying the long-term needs of all major stakeholders—students, faculty and staff, parents, employers, and taxpayers—in our colleges and universities.

In short, we need an overarching purpose of a college education that cuts across general education and specialization as well as fields of study ranging from the liberal arts and sciences to professional fields of study—all the while accommodating mission differentiation. Such an overarching and transparent purpose can guide undergraduate education—from curricular requirements and course design to the extracurriculum, our teaching practices, and above all the learning experiences of our students—in ways that help to ensure that our college graduates are prepared for far more than the short-term, transient workplace.

part three

Becoming an Inquiry-Driven Learner

chapter four

Portrayal of an Inquiry-Driven Learner

Merlin, King Arthur's mentor, offered this bit of wisdom in *The Once and Future King:*

> [To] learn something. That is the only thing that never fails. You may grow old and trembling in your anatomies, you may lie awake at night listening to the disorder of your veins, . . . you may see the world around you devastated by evil lunatics, or know your honor trampled in the sewers of baser minds. There is only one thing for it then—to learn. . . . That is the only thing which the mind can never exhaust, never alienate, never be tortured by, never fear or distrust, and never dream of regretting. Learning is the thing for you. (White, 1987, p. 183)

In this chapter we advance our idea of the purpose of a college education in the twenty-first century: to educate *inquiry-driven learners.* The concept of an inquiry-driven learner is anchored in the premise that the twenty-first century landscape is one in which change—cultural, economic, political, interpersonal, environmental—has become the defining feature. From our personal spaces to our places of work, our communities, our nation-state, and across the globe, change and uncertainty affect us all. Ronald Barnett (2005, p. 789) refers to our world as one of "unpredictability" and "strangeness," and Joshua Ramo (2009) calls it an "age of surprise." We think of it as an "age of uncertainty."

Regardless of how it is labeled, the world in which we live—from the local to the global level—needs individuals who are able to address successfully not only anticipated but also unanticipated challenges and opportunities. In the ever-changing global workplace, creative and disciplined problem-solvers are sorely needed—people who can adapt to changing workplaces and generate innovative ideas. No less important, citizens need to be able to navigate uncharted territory in their lives beyond the workplace. In order to be relevant, higher education needs to prepare students to pursue ideas across all aspects of their lives—from the workplace, to their public engagement, to their personal lives. As poignantly expressed by Vartan Gregorian, "We must remind ourselves that the value of a . . . [college] education and education in general is to enhance people's powers of rational analysis, intellectual precision, independent judgment, and mental adaptability. . . . Education must make us more than well-ordered puppets in the passing show, making gestures with no sense of the significance of the human drama, moved only by the strings that tie us to material things" (Hersh & Merrow, 2005, p. 80).

We begin this chapter by introducing our concept of an inquiry-driven learner. In the remainder of the chapter we elaborate on the four signature capabilities of an inquiry-driven learner.

Definition of an Inquiry-Driven Learner

We define an *inquiry-driven learner* as a person who has the capability to explore and cultivate promising ideas—ideas that will enable him or her to successfully navigate constant change and capitalize on career opportunities, enjoy his or her personal life, and thoughtfully engage in public life.[1] Most definitions of a college-educated person place primary emphasis on becoming "learned" *as an end in itself*—that is, the end of a college education is the acquisition of a requisite body of knowledge and skills, whether for the workplace, one's public life, or one's personal life. In contrast, the purpose we advance makes becoming a "learner" the endpoint.[2] We propose that the hallmark of educated persons is not that they have acquired a body of broad-based and job-specific knowledge and skills but that they have the capabilities to pursue promising ideas with imagination and discipline, whether pursued for their own sake or for direct application to real-world problems.[3] Our focus on *learner* rather than *learned-ness* is anchored in an observation made by Eric Hoffer: "In times of change, the LEARNERS shall inherit the earth, while the learned find themselves beautifully equipped to deal with a world that no longer exists" (Proctor, 2007, pp. xiii–xiv).

An inquiry-driven learner has four signature capabilities: (1) core qualities of mind, (2) critical thinking skills, (3) expertise in divergent modes of inquiry, and (4) the capacity to express and communicate ideas. The figure on page 62 provides a visual representation of these four capabilities.

The first of these capabilities encompasses six core qualities of mind that propel and inform the search for promising ideas: explore ideas with enthusiasm and meet challenges with resilience; embrace ownership in the pursuit of ideas; question self, extant knowledge, and authorities; engage in spirited dialogue and collaboration; contemplate; and commit to inquiry on behalf of self, society, and humanity.

We define critical thinking skills—the second capability—as those rational processes of thought associated with making sound inferences, interpretations, and judgments based on persuasive evidence and sound reasoning. We accentuate three critical thinking skills: frame burning questions; access, comprehend, and dialogue with extant knowledge; and analyze, synthesize, and interpret knowledge and information.

The third capability is expertise in at least two divergent modes of inquiry (ways of knowing). Rather than being inundated with conventional content knowledge per se—such as learning to weep with Achilles, becoming familiar with the fault lines in Darwin's (1859) *On the Origin of Species by Means of Natural Selection,* or memorizing which presidents of the United States served as generals in the armed forces—an inquiry-driven learner has the capacity to apply divergent approaches to problem-solving and pursue inquiry as a dynamic and recursive experience. The last of the four capabilities is the capacity to express and communicate ideas—especially the ability to transform ideas into language and, in turn, communicate them to other people. Below we elaborate on each of the capabilities, beginning with the six core qualities of mind.[4]

Core Qualities of Mind
- Explore Ideas with Enthusiasm and meet Challenges with Resilience
- Embrace Ownership in the Pursuit of Ideas
- Question Self, Extant Knowlege, and Authorities
- Engage in Spirited Dialogue and Collaboration
- Contemplate
- Commit to Inquiry on Behalf of Self, Society, and Humanity

Capacity to Express and Communicate Ideas
- Transform Ideas into Language
- Communicate Ideas through Writing and Speaking

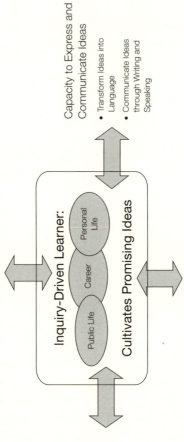

Inquiry-Driven Learner:

Public Life Career Personal Life

Cultivates Promising Ideas

Critical Thinking Skills
- Frame Burning Questions
- Access, Understand, and Dialogue with Extant Knowledge
- Analyze, Synthesize, and Interpret Knowledge and Information

Expertise in Divergent Modes of Inquiry
- Apply Divergent Approaches to Problem-Solving
- Pursue Inquiry as a Dynamic and Recursive Experience

Graphic representation of an inquiry-driven learner

Core Qualities of Mind

Six core qualities of mind—each of which cuts across cognitive, af-fective, and ethical domains—at once propel and inform the search for promising ideas in the rapidly changing, interconnected, and uncertain world in which we live. These qualities provide the foun-dation for inquiry-driven learners in their pursuit of meaningful ideas.

Explore Ideas with Enthusiasm and Meet Challenges with Resilience

At the core of an inquiry-driven learner is a passion for pursuing ideas. Inspired by what Albert Einstein referred to as a "holy curios-ity," an inquiry-driven learner embodies enthusiasm that is fueled by curiosity and the joy—a simple, unspeakable joy—found in the pur-suit of ideas. Along with animating their inquiry, this exuberance often leads inquiry-driven learners to appreciate that the curiosity of others can be a powerful source of inspiration and, in turn, can lead to the pursuit of ideas that matter not only to oneself but also to other people, society, and humanity at large.

The curiosity of individuals is often diminished through socializa-tion and traditional schooling. As they grow older, children who once read books with pleasure and wrote with fluency begin to struggle with those same activities. They may encounter socialization prac-tices in which they are ridiculed for expressing perspectives that fall outside of the status quo. When teachers with measuring rods up their sleeves expect their students to become skilled at rote memorization and to regurgitate information, enthusiasm for learning and the cre-ative spirit is often diminished, as students increasingly distrust their own voices and lose interest in engaging the questions about which they are curious. Notwithstanding such challenges, inquiry-driven learners are resilient in their pursuit of ideas. Such perseverance is essential, not least in a world in which curiosity is often frowned upon and in which we often are surrounded by individuals who bring mes-sianic certainty to both public and private discourse. Inquiry-driven learners meet rigidity of thought with courage and resilience, persevering even in the face of ridicule.

Whether one embraces a "mad scientist" approach to inquiry or an inspired search for ideas as embodied in the work of the poet Wendell Berry, inquiry-driven learners are adventurers who bolster their enthusiasm for learning and their resilience with an appreciation that, in the words of John Steinbeck, "Ideas are like rabbits. You get a couple and learn how to handle them, and pretty soon you have a dozen" (van Gelder, 1947, p. 123).

Embrace Ownership in the Pursuit of Ideas

Anchored in their passion to pursue ideas, inquiry-driven learners seize ownership of their inquiry. This sense of ownership begins internally; its domain spreads from the inside out, not from the outside in. Once catalyzed, inquiry-driven learners not only search for new ideas with enthusiasm, but they take personal responsibility to be creative, thoughtful, and disciplined in their inquiry. By maintaining ownership over their inquiry and the corollary proposition that their inquiry matters, inquiry-driven learners seize the initiative to hone their ideas. As active rather than passive learners, they nourish other capabilities, such as the higher-order thinking skills of analysis, synthesis, and interpretation.

Question Self, Extant Knowledge, and Authorities

Inquiry-driven learners respectfully question not only their own predispositions—including the filters through which they process new information—but also existing literature, conventional wisdom, and the perspectives of authorities. In so doing, they challenge their own viewpoints and perspectives, along with those of others, as they sift and winnow through ideas in dogged pursuit of truth. They give reason to believe, in the words of H. L. Mencken, that individuals become learners "not in proportion to their willingness to believe, but in proportion to their readiness to doubt" (1930, p. 153). Inquiry-driven learners exhibit Jacob Bronowski's admonition that students "bring a certain ragamuffin barefoot irreverence to their studies; they are not here to worship what is known, but to question it (1973, p. 360).

Questioning self, existing knowledge, and authorities stands in sharp contrast to the uncompromising certainty that often surrounds us. How often do we find ourselves in an unceasing flow of information, from the 24-hour news stations that seem to dictate the opinions and beliefs that right-minded individuals must adopt, to humor-based news entertainment that often does little more than mock established institutions? Inquiry-driven learners develop the capacity to distance themselves from the information that surrounds them, at once challenging received truths and trusting their own ability to pursue more compelling truths—even when faced with pressure to accept uncritically the perspectives and norms of others.

By questioning extant knowledge, conventional wisdom, authorities, and their own predispositions, inquiry-driven learners are far more likely to imbue the search for new ideas with imagination and creativity. From deciding what questions to pursue and how to pursue their guiding questions, inquiry-driven learners question their own information-processing skills while simultaneously challenging the ideas they are engaged in developing.

Engage in Spirited Dialogue and Collaboration

An inquiry-driven learner engages in spirited dialogue and collaboration with other people. In the words of Michel de Montaigne, "We may whet and sharpen our wits by rubbing them against those of others" (1877). To that end, as they engage in the ongoing process of sorting through ideas, inquiry-driven learners seek out individuals with differing and contrarian perspectives who are able, and willing, to engage in spirited dialogue. Through dialogue, inquiry-driven learners embody a healthy skepticism that, at the same time, is accompanied by genuine respect for, and openness to, the perspectives, values, and beliefs of other people. Engaging in dialogue gives inquiry-driven learners opportunities to test their thinking and can bring imagination and creativity to their pursuit of ideas.

Inquiry-driven learners greatly appreciate the potential of collaboration to enlarge the scope of their inquiry, recognizing that ideas may be greatly enriched by the perspectives of other people. As they interact with others, they may decide to reframe their questions, pursue new lines of reasoning, or altogether throw out understandings they previously held. This willingness to collaborate, while assessing and recalibrating, is a hallmark of the courage necessary to become an inquiry-driven learner, and it can also increase the likelihood that the ideas being advanced will benefit not only the individuals involved but the greater good as well. To be sure, spirited dialogue often calls for a good measure of courage. By asking questions, inquiry-driven learners take risks that sometimes make them, and others, uncomfortable. They persist nonetheless—all the while being respectful of the perspectives of others.

Contemplate

Whether by questioning extant knowledge and new information, framing questions, conducting inquiry, or transforming ideas into language, an inquiry-driver learner engages in contemplation. Taking the time to contemplate—stepping out of the frenetic stream of daily activity in order to pause and reflect—is central to the search for promising ideas. Contemplation is precious, not least in a world in which technology is omnipresent and solitude must be sought with diligence. An inquiry-driver learner appreciates as much. For the challenges of the workplace, personal life, and public involvement are often complex and unpredictable, and taking the time and the energy to reflect is critical to pursuing ideas. Indeed, the act of contemplation provides an opportunity to question oneself, thereby inviting both creativity and disciplined thought. In short, an inquiry-driven learner is vigilant in maintaining fidelity to the dictum of Confucius: "Learning without thought is labor lost" (1998, p. 18).

To maintain sacred spaces for contemplation, inquiry-driven learners purposefully consider, rather than immediately react to, the constant flow of information that resides no farther away than the smart phone at their fingertips. Many technological devices demand immediate attention and quick action, variously peppering inquiry-driven learners with sounds, vibrations, alarms, and updates. Thoughtless response to each ping can result in frenetic activity that interrupts thought, undermines inquiry, halts careful reflection, dams up inspiration, thwarts rational analysis, and defers reflection. Accordingly, the inquiry-driven learner carefully manages communication modes and technologies, recognizing that while these tools can greatly enrich inquiry they can also be highly distracting in the search for promising ideas.

Commit to Inquiry on Behalf of Self, Society, and Humanity

Along with an enthusiasm for pursuing ideas, inquiry-driven learners are committed to engaging in inquiry that is fired by a passion for enriching not only themselves but also society and humanity at large. While the importance of engaging in inquiry to enhance one's own life is obvious, less obvious is a lifetime commitment to developing ideas that contribute to the lives of others—from family and friends, to neighbors and community, to nation-state and the global community. An inquiry-driven learner embraces an ethic of responsibility to self and others through generating and communicating ideas that contribute to the greater good. John Gardner, Secretary of the former U.S. Department of Health, Education, and Welfare, described the underlying social contract in a democracy this way: "Freedom and responsibility, liberty and duty, that's the deal" (O'Connell, 2005, p. 199). Why such a deal? Drawing from antiquity, Edith Hamilton suggested a more fundamental reason: "If men insist on being free from the burden of [responsibility] for the common good they . . . cease to be free at all. Responsibility [is] the price every man must pay for freedom" (1957, p. 47).

Why should inquiry-driven learners care about the common good? The human species is interconnected. By recognizing and appreciating that we live in a global world in which we are all more or less mutually dependent, inquiry-driven learners reach beyond themselves in their pursuit of ideas. Indeed, such a commitment ought to be at the forefront of much of their inquiry, for if we are to survive as individuals and as a species we need to develop ideas that help us not just individually but also across numerous planes of human existence. From melting glaciers and depleted rainforests, to diminishing fresh water supplies and the constant threat of terrorism and nuclear weapons, humanity needs ideas that serve the greater good.

Finally, inquiry-driven learners both understand and appreciate that their inquiry matters more as they reach beyond themselves—for their ideas may positively affect other people. From researchers seeking to cure epilepsy or cancer, to government leaders seeking to prevent terrorist acts and sustain water supplies, inquiry-driven learners strive to reach beyond themselves. And those who pursue inquiry in service to the common good are apt to exhibit relatively high levels of resilience, doggedness, and persistence in their inquiry because they appreciate that other people rely upon them to succeed.

Critical Thinking Skills

Critical thinking skills comprise the second capability of an inquiry-driven learner. In broad strokes, we define critical thinking skills as the ability to bring new ideas to fruition using rational processes of thought that are grounded in credible evidence and sound reasoning. More specifically, critical thinking skills are those skills that enable inquiry-driven learners to frame their inquiry and to pursue and harness ideas with thoughtfulness and rigor.

Three critical thinking skills fuel inquiry-driven learners. These include the abilities to (1) frame burning questions; (2) access, understand, and dialogue with extant knowledge; and (3) interpret, analyze, and synthesize knowledge and information. Although we present these skills sequentially, they are highly interdependent, with the ability to frame burning questions serving at once to energize and sustain the two other critical thinking skills.

Frame Burning Questions

Inquiry-driven learners are able to frame burning questions—in the workplace, in public, and in their private lives. For the purpose of reinforcing the centrality of the burning question to her students, the psychologist Susan Harter (2006, p. 331) displays the following mantra on her office wall: "What is your burning question?" Why is the ability to developing burning questions critical to exemplary inquiry? Albert Einstein responded to the latter question in this way: "The mere formulation of a problem is far more often essential than its solution, which may be merely a matter of mathematical or experimental skill. To raise new questions, new possibilities, to regard longstanding problems from a new angle requires creative imagination and makes real advances in science" (Einstein & Infeld, 1938, p. 92). Indeed, because many of the most formidable challenges and opportunities in our lives have not yet been identified, the capacity to frame burning questions is especially critical in the rapidly changing world of the twenty-first century. Instead of wandering aimlessly through reams of data and information, inquiry-driven learners use burning questions to target the scope of inquiry and inform their search for promising ideas.

In arriving at questions to guide their inquiry, inquiry-driven learners trust their own intellects, choosing to pursue questions about which they are passionate—questions that "burn" for them. If a question does not "burn," people engaged in inquiry are likely to become disengaged, thereby self-silencing their sources of creativity and inspiration. Their human potential has been stemmed because they have given ownership of the question to someone else, or to some extant data, rather than trusting the passion and fire that they, themselves, have about questions that are meaningful to them.

When individuals pursue questions about which they are passionate, their passion engenders a sense of ownership not only in terms of formulating their guiding questions but also throughout the course of their inquiry. Simply stated, if one cares about something, then one owns it. To be sure, taking ownership over the questions that guide one's inquiry can involve risk-taking. Other people may be uncomfortable with the questions being asked, for such questions may be a threat to the status quo. Still, inquiry-driven learners persist because their burning questions are important to them.

Just as inquiry-driven learners are neither held hostage by questions others have sought to have answered nor intimidated in the face of resistance, they also learn to question their own initial take on a problem. They therefore remain open to modifying their burning questions during the course of their inquiry. Inquiry-driven learners are willing to change, recalibrate, and adjust their burning questions in response to new data, information, and occurrences as they arise.

Access, Understand, and Dialogue with Extant Knowledge and Information

In tandem with identifying questions that "burn" for them, inquiry-driven learners appreciate that their burning questions provide them with a ready filter for accessing relevant knowledge and information during their inquiry. Recognizing that their search for promising ideas can be enriched by studying the work of others, inquiry-driven learners actively engage knowledge and information and dialogue with it.

Inquiry does not stop once information has been accessed and understood, for inquiry-driven learners engage extant knowledge and information instead of simply absorbing it. Guided by their burning question, they dialogue with the knowledge and information that they access and reflect on how it may be relevant to and enrich their inquiry. For example, when reading a published article, rather than only asking themselves, "What does the author's research mean?" they also ask, "In what ways might this author's research matter to my burning question?" How might their approach to collecting and analyzing information be of use in my own search for understanding?" In this manner, rather than resigning power over to existing sources of knowledge and information, inquiry-driven learners dialogue with the subject matter they encounter. Through this dialogue—in effect, an ongoing "conversation" about the relevance of information—their inquiry may be markedly enriched and enlarged as existing knowledge is challenged.

Interpret, Analyze, and Synthesize Knowledge and Information

It is not enough for inquiry-driven learners to access and understand extant knowledge and information. They must also be able to interpret, analyze, and synthesize what they take from diverse sources in order to crystallize burning questions and pursue them with imagination and discipline. In brief, interpretation is the ability to transform extant knowledge and new information and integrate it into an existing body of knowledge. Through this process, inquiry-driven learners build upon existing knowledge and enrich their pursuit of new ideas.

Analysis refers to an inquiry-driven learner's ability to break apart extant knowledge and information into discrete categories. Visualize, for example, disassembling a 500-piece jigsaw puzzle—the 500 pieces of the puzzle would be separated so that each individual piece stood as a discrete piece upon a table. By analogy, analysis empowers inquiry-driven learners to disassemble the knowledge and information they access, carefully teasing out discrete pieces. But unlike the disassembly of a puzzle, by which preordained puzzle pieces are separated, inquiry-driven learners are able to break apart extant knowledge into the shapes and sizes that best serve their pursuit of ideas.

Through the process of synthesis, inquiry-driven learners fuse the new categories they have teased out through analysis of extant knowledge and information. In short, to synthesize is to bring pieces of information together in innovative ways and unify them into a coherent and meaningful whole. By so doing, inquiry-driven learners have the ability to imaginatively recast knowledge and information in new ways, as well as break apart old paradigms in order to fully actualize the potential of their inquiry.[5]

Expertise in Divergent Modes of Inquiry

As we proposed in our chapter on the default purpose of an undergraduate education, a focus on "knowledge acquisition" fails to appreciate that, in the uncertain world in which we live, individuals must first and foremost be able to develop ideas that will prepare them to meet the rapid and continuing change that awaits them in the workplace as well as in their personal and public endeavors. Accordingly, we propose a shift away from the dominant emphasis on the *acquisition of content knowledge* (which is widely reflected in conventional general education requirements), and instead, we place major emphasis on cultivating *expertise in divergent modes of inquiry* (ways of knowing). Put simply, we envision inquiry-driven learners as individuals who, having studied and engaged in inquiry in two or more divergent disciplines or interdisciplinary fields of study, have honed their capacity to draw upon divergent modes of inquiry in their pursuit of ideas. Specifically, inquiry-driven learners have the capability to apply divergent approaches to problem-solving and the capability to pursue inquiry as a dynamic and recursive experience.

Apply Divergent Approaches to Problem-Solving

In their search for and testing of ideas, inquiry-driven learners are able to draw upon divergent approaches to inquiry and knowledge generation. More specifically, they understand and make use of the norms, methods, and techniques associated with at least two different approaches to inquiry. For example, students who have developed expertise in scientific and humanistic modes of inquiry in such fields as botany and philosophy know not only what constitutes "scientific inquiry" and rhetorical analysis but also how to conduct it. Closely related, inquiry-driven learners have developed proficiency with respect to the conduct and representation of inquiry in a range of fields and subfields, from the humanities (such as philosophy, art history, Spanish) and the social sciences (such as psychology, political science, sociology) to professional fields of study (such as social work, theater and drama, elementary education) and interdisciplinary studies (such as international studies, wildlife ecology, environmental studies).

Inquiry-driven learners also have learned to experiment with various tools that can support problem-solving. For example, they may have used lab protocols; learned to interpret cultural artifacts; and participated in study groups, wikis, listservs, and blogs. In so doing, they have learned that inquiry which leads to promising ideas is often characterized by discontinuity and confusion, and they are able at once to address that discontinuity and generate ideas—including ideas that defy conventional expectations. Having learned to be open to points of discontinuity and surprise throughout their inquiry, they are able to reconsider the questions they are asking, the data that capture their attention, and the inferences they are making. Such metacognitive abilities—which often are at the heart of first-rate inquiry—enable inquiry-driven learners to refocus their inquiry, stop and restart it, modify questions and advance their ideas as the inquiry unfolds. And not least, these learners appreciate that discontinuity and being open to surprise often foster creativity in the search for promising ideas.

Pursue Inquiry as Dynamic and Recursive Experience

An inquiry-driven learner pursues ideas in much the same way that professionals take on a problem, engaging in what Donald Schön called "reflection-in-action" (1987, p. xi). An inquiry-driven learner does not see an existing field of inquiry as an a priori set of problems, solutions, and tolerances but as a site of action—a space in which to frame burning questions, develop context-specific ways of addressing those questions, and then analyze and report findings. By pursuing ideas through "reflection-in-action," an inquiry-driven learner develops a sensory awareness of how it feels to arrive at productive questions and how to pose follow-up questions in the pursuit of those questions that guide their inquiry.

More often than not, individuals with expertise in divergent modes of inquiry have enhanced their capacity for inquiry by working alongside experienced inquirers. For as a complex process itself, inquiry is perhaps best learned in a kind of apprenticeship with individuals who personify and embody both discipline and imagination in the pursuit of ideas within their respective domains of inquiry. To illustrate, inquiry-driven learners who specialize in anthropology might engage in inquiry with an anthropology professor who invites them to visit a study site and take field notes. In short, inquiry-driven learners have learned that inquiry is much more than simply memorizing and then applying rules to a problem space. They understand and appreciate that robust inquiry is a dynamic and recursive experience.

The Capacity to Express and Communicate Ideas

The capacity to express and communicate ideas—in particular, transforming ideas into language and communicating them—is essential. Absent this capacity, ideas remain dormant, undeveloped, and without impact. Significantly, while the creation and effective communication of ideas may occur in sequence, harnessing language to communicate ideas is frequently a highly dynamic process that requires careful development. Below we elaborate on the capability of transforming ideas from thought into language, and thereafter, the capability to communicate them in writing and in speaking.

Transform Ideas into Language

Having ideas unexpressed is equivalent to having no ideas at all. As Pericles put it, "He who cannot express what he thinks is at the level of he who does not think" (Booth & Thornley-Hall, 1991, p. 66). Needless to say, it can be challenging to transform nascent ideas into a form of expression that can be fully understood by oneself as well as other people. While there are many compelling ways to express ideas—from art and music to theater and dance—we propose that an inquiry-driven learner must above all be able to transform ideas into language. We emphasize language on the grounds that it is a universal tool and, further, that the ability to express ideas in language is often a critical test of the quality of ideas. As J. Michael Straczynski wrote, "The quality of our thought is bordered on all sides by our facility with language" (BenShea, 2000, p. 112).

In developing ideas and transforming them into language, inquiry-driven learners "play" with the ideas running through their mind, creatively casting and recasting them in new ways; reflecting deeply on them; and ultimately giving them expression in words. Inquiry-driven learners use language to give full and robust expression to the ideas they are pursuing.

Communicate Ideas through Writing and Speaking

The ability to communicate ideas is as important as transforming one's ideas from thought into language. For ideas that are not shared with other people are not likely to positively shape either an inquiry-driven learner's life—personally, professionally, or publicly—or the lives of others. Thus, inquiry-driven learners recognize and appreciate that sharing ideas reflects an ethic of responsibility to society and humanity as well as to themselves. Moreover, they are able to communicate their ideas in both speech and writing in a manner that is tailored to their intended audience. Depending upon their audience, they may contribute to Facebook pages or blogs on websites, establish themselves in online communities, and ultimately open new opportunities for dialogue; or they may focus on academic scholarship, perhaps coauthoring papers with faculty, where their goal is to advance ideas within a specific field of study. In short, inquiry-driven learners understand the nature of their audience and tailor both the content and communication of their ideas to that audience.

Building upon a Legacy of Ideas

Our concept of an inquiry-driven learner draws on the ideas of many who have preceded us, from the notion of "inquiry" to the four capabilities that are the foundation of inquiry-driven learning. Numerous individuals have made references in their writings to "learners" and "inquiry," but we have been particularly influenced by the writings of Michael Oakeshott and John Dewey, as well as the problem-based learning (PBL) movement within higher education.

Michael Oakeshott, the British political philosopher, has written extensively on education. In a collection of his writings edited by Timothy Fuller (1989, p. 24), Oakeshott wrote: "The distinctive feature of . . . a special place of learning is, first, that those who occupy it are recognized and recognize themselves pre-eminently as learners." Oakeshott's writings—scholarship that goes far beyond the platitudes of those who use such well-intentioned but empty phrases as "life-long learning" and "broad-based education"—heavily influenced our decision to place "learners" alongside our concept of "inquiry-driven." Thus, we unified them, placing those concepts at the center of the purpose of a college education that we have proposed.

The writings of John Dewey also have had a major influence on our emphasis on inquiry. Dewey (1938) proposed the creation of K-12 schools that connected school learning with the life experiences of students through "problem-solving," which helped prepare them for their future in the workforce and as citizens. In underscoring learning by doing, Dewey emphasized that schooling "must be derived from materials which at the outset fall within the scope of ordinary life-experience" (p. 73). His scholarship influenced our vision in two major ways: one, by emphasizing the importance of linking learning to the "real world," and two, by placing problem-solving at or near the center of education—which is reflected not least in our emphasis on preparing college graduates for their civic and personal lives as well as their careers.

While John Dewey's influence is found primarily in K-12 education, his work has had a significant impact on the development of the problem-based learning (PBL) movement in higher education and, in turn, on our proposed purpose. Problem-based learning is a "learner-centered method" aimed at educating independent learners who are prepared to address the problems they encounter throughout their lives. While this focus on problem-solving has influenced our thinking, problem-based learning differs from our proposed purpose. Most important, PBL places more emphasis on acquiring, recalling, and applying "learned information." In contrast, we place considerably less emphasis on the acquisition and application of extant knowledge than on the continuing search for knowledge and understanding; incorporate a more inclusive range of critical thinking skills; and place major emphasis on the importance of acquiring expertise in divergent modes of inquiry. Caveats aside, the work of John Dewey—and such initiatives as the PBL movement in higher education—have had a significant impact on our development of the purpose we have proposed.[6]

Other writings have also had a major impact on the capabilities incorporated into our fundamental purpose of a college education. Albeit as ends and not as means, these capabilities reach back to the ancient liberal arts tradition. The concept of "qualities-of-mind" can be traced back to ancient Greece, though various other terms have been used over the centuries—such as "attitudes of mind" and "habits of mind." The concept of "critical thinking skills" goes back to the Greco-Roman period and to Aristotle in particular. More than a half-century ago, Benjamin Bloom and his colleagues advanced two widely cited taxonomies of educational objectives—namely, a cognitive taxonomy (Bloom et al., 1956) and an affective taxonomy (Krathwohl, Bloom & Masia, 1999)—with the cognitive taxonomy having a direct impact on the capability we refer to as "critical thinking skills," specifically our emphasis on "analysis" and "synthesis." Although the Yale Report of 1828, with its emphases on "discipline of the mind" and "habits of mind," no doubt influenced our emphasis on critical thinking skills and qualities of mind, our purpose differs in major ways. For example, the specific critical thinking skills and qualities of mind that we elaborate are more often than not very different from those cited in the Yale Report. Most noteworthy, our "core qualities of mind" have relatively little in common with previous attempts to identify "habits of mind" or attitudes of mind. These capabilities are, we repeat, means and not ends in our vision: becoming learned is not the end in our guiding purpose; becoming an inquiry-driven learner is.

Building upon and extending this legacy of ideas, we have advanced the concept of an inquiry-driven learner. As we have defined and elaborated on this concept, an inquiry-driven learner is a person who has the capability to explore and cultivate promising ideas that will enable him or her to navigate the rapid change in the world of the twenty-first century—in the workplace and in his or her personal and public lives.

Imagine that every college and university graduate had not only the core qualities of mind of an inquiry-driven learner but the other three signature capabilities as well: critical thinking skills, expertise in divergent modes of inquiry, and the capacity to express and communicate ideas. If we in higher education are to prepare students for an uncertain future, what better way to educate them than to nourish their capabilities in ways that will enrich the major domains of their lives, including their workplace lives, their public engagement, and their personal lives?

With respect to the workplace, educating students to pursue ideas with imagination and discipline in their professional lives will prepare them to come up with innovative ideas and engage in creative and disciplined problem-solving in areas ranging from the technical and bureaucratic to highly complex substantive matters. Moreover, consonant with Steven Cahn's argument in *Education and the Democratic Ideal* (1979)—an argument advanced by many others (Dewey, [1916] 1967; Miller, 1988; Westbrook, 1991) as well—what better way to prepare people to assume an active and thoughtful role as contributors to our democracy than to equip them with core qualities of mind that enable them to engage in spirited dialogue and collaboration, reflect and contemplate, and engage critical thinking skills that enable them to analyze, synthesize, and interpret knowledge and information and effectively express and communicate ideas through writing and speaking? And with respect to the frequent adaptation and creative problem-solving that can shape their personal lives, can there be a better way to prepare our students than to foster in them core qualities of mind, critical thinking skills, expertise in divergent modes of inquiry, and the capacity to express and communicate that are at the center of an inquiry-driven learner?

Our colleges and universities have formidable resources for preparing students as individuals, citizens, and workers for the twenty-first-century world of rapid change, diversity, and uncertainty. Higher education's longstanding focus on inquiry can significantly contribute to that preparation, provided that inquiry is emphasized not only by professors and graduate students but also by undergraduate students, whose focus on becoming inquiry-driven learners must extend far beyond becoming learned. The purpose of a college education advanced here—placing inquiry-driven learning at the heart of undergraduate education—holds the promise of inspiring individuals across higher learning and empowering undergraduate students to live richer lives in a world where change is constant and the ground on which they stand is always shifting.

part four

Developing Inquiry-Driven Learners

chapter five

Ideas for Developing Inquiry-Driven Learners

In this book we have argued that in the rapidly changing, interconnected, and uncertain world of the twenty-first century there is an urgent need for a compelling purpose of an undergraduate education that can be widely shared across our colleges and universities. In turn, we have advanced an overarching purpose that is centered on developing graduates who have the capacity to explore and cultivate ideas that will prepare them to capitalize upon career opportunities, enrich their personal lives, and thoughtfully participate in public life.

Drawing on a wide range of contemporary practices in colleges and universities in the United States, in this concluding chapter we identify institutional initiatives and practices for educating inquiry-driven learners. The chapter is divided into two sections. The first explores initiatives at eight American colleges and universities of varying sizes and missions, all of which are variously cultivating inquiry-driven learners across the undergraduate experience. The second distills a range of institutional practices for developing inquiry-driven learners within three parallel planes: (1) the teaching and learning that occurs in the classroom, in online interactions, and in research activities; (2) the structure of courses; and (3) university mission statements, policies, and strategic planning processes.

Initiatives at Eight Institutions

To identify institutional initiatives that are in harmony with our proposed purpose of a college education, we engaged in a two-step process. As an initial screening device, we employed multiple sources—

including college and university catalogs, websites, scholarly literature, media, and personal contacts. We then identified more than 200 curricular and teaching initiatives that aligned with our concept of the "inquiry-driven learner."[1] Second, we studied the goals and key features of many of these initiatives to determine if they were not only focused on preparing "inquirers" but also tethered to at least three of the four capacities of an inquiry-driven learner.

In light of this process, we chose to highlight eight initiatives. The first five initiatives are aimed at integrating inquiry-driven learning practices across the entire undergraduate curriculum. They include the inquiry-based undergraduate curriculum at the Evergreen State College, a public liberal arts college; the undergraduate curriculum at the Worcester Polytechnic University; the interdisciplinary and experiential learning undergraduate curriculum at the New Century College at George Mason University, a small experimental college housed within a large public university; an "inquiry-guided learning" initiative at North Carolina State University; and three pockets of innovation in the undergraduate curriculum at the University of Wisconsin–Madison. The three remaining initiatives are more modest in scope, encompassing a single year in college, a single program, or a single resource that is widely available to both students and faculty. These initiatives include the Collaborative Undergraduate Research and Inquiry Program at St. Olaf College; the Freshman Learning Project at Indiana University Bloomington; and the Critical Thinking Skills resource housed at the University of New Mexico College of Nursing.[2]

Housed in institutions with remarkably different missions and institutional identities, including research universities, liberal arts colleges, urban universities, and regional colleges, these diverse initiatives illustrate that inquiry-driven learners can be developed in myriad ways, which can be adjusted to the needs, interests, actors, and missions of all kinds of institutions. And not insignificantly, as many of the initiatives highlighted in this chapter suggest, inquiry-driven leaning can be implemented with relatively modest curricular overhaul and at reasonable expense.

The Evergreen State College: An Inquiry-Based Undergraduate Curriculum

The Evergreen State College is a public liberal arts institution located in Olympia, Washington, that has long been known for its innovative program offerings at the undergraduate level. It provides a distinctive curricular model for other institutions to reflect on if they are considering the introduction of inquiry-driven teaching and learning practices across the entire undergraduate curriculum.

The mission of the Evergreen State College is to sustain a vibrant academic community that offers students an education that helps them to excel in their intellectual, creative, professional, and community service endeavors. Anchored in this mission are five specific foci that serve as the basis for curriculum development: (1) Interdisciplinary Study: Evergreen students learn to synthesize ideas and concepts from many subject areas, enhancing their capacity to solve real-world problems; (2) Collaborative Learning: students develop knowledge and skills through shared learning experiences, rather than learning in isolation or in competition with others; (3) Learning across Significant Differences: students learn to recognize, respect, and bridge differences with others, thereby enhancing critical thinking skills as well as understanding and appreciating others in an increasingly diverse world; (4) Personal Engagement: students develop their capacities to conduct inquiry, write, speak, and act on the basis of their own reasoned beliefs while simultaneously engaging and respecting the beliefs of others; and (5) Linking Theory with Practical Applications: students learn to apply abstract theories in practice in real-life situations, such as taking internships with prospective employers and engaging in public service with nonprofit organizations.[3]

Along with these five foci, a signature hallmark of the undergraduate curriculum at Evergreen is the structure of its academic programs. Students do not enroll in courses across multiple, sectioned-off academic disciplines, as is the case at most colleges and universities. Instead, Evergreen students enroll in a single academic program each semester—a program that is both interdisciplinary and collaborative and through which they explore a central idea or theme that integrates divergent academic disciplines. Over the course of a single semester, or several successive semesters, a student might study problems in health care from the points of view of biology, history, philosophy, sociology, economics, and literature, or they might study the physical world through the interplay of physics, chemistry, philosophy, and mathematics.

Each program enrolls about 25 students in a learning community that includes reading assignments, lectures, labs, seminars, field study, and research projects. Programs last from one to three quarters and build successively on themes developed in prior quarters. Faculty members from several different disciplines collaboratively teach each academic program in teams of two to four, with each professor drawing on several disciplines to assist students in framing their burning questions and enhancing their higher-order thinking skills in pursuing real-world problems across multiple disciplines.

Students in Evergreen's learning communities also collaborate in conducting inquiry, engage in spirited dialogue, share their ideas with one another, explain their ideas in written and oral presentations, and apply their ideas in laboratories and public workshops. Moreover, faculty encourage students to comprehend and dialogue with existing knowledge and respectfully challenge their own and others' ideas, all the while taking ownership over and assuming responsibility for their own learning and personal growth.

Each year, Evergreen students prepare an Academic Plan, which they discuss with faculty and, in so doing, take responsibility for planning their learning experiences and academic careers. They also learn to bridge theory and practice by working for businesses, public agencies, and nonprofit organizations or by developing internships that allow them to apply their skills in workplace settings. Two examples of academic programs at Evergreen State College include a program entitled "500 Years of Globalization" and another called "Music, Math, and Motion."[4] Each is briefly discussed below.

The globalization program cuts across the disciplines of geography, history, political science, international studies, and sociology. In light of major shifts in political, economic, and geostrategic power on a global scale, students enrolled in this program have engaged in inquiry related to such topics as the hypermobility of capital, the reemergence of nationalism, the increasing disparity and similarity between first and third world countries, the relationship between transnational corporations and multilateral institutions, and the changing structures of power under the current crisis in global capitalism. The globalization program challenges students to apply divergent modes of inquiry by drawing on the fields of history, geography, and sociology. To illustrate, students simultaneously engage in the study of the evolution of historical capitalism, the international political economy, and the social structures through which Europeans and Euro-Americans created capitalism, the nation-state, redrew the world map through colonialism and imperialism, and established international rules of commerce over the past 500 years.

The "Music, Math, and Motion" program is designed for students who find their art increasingly mediated by technology, for students who seek an artistic outlet within their pursuit of science, and for students interested in the interweaving of art and science. To that end, the program integrates multiple ways of understanding music and technology by integrating the study of mathematics, physics, music, and art. It builds on the synergy between mathematics and physics in ways that use language to describe existing worlds, as well as the synergy between music and art. The divergent modes of inquiry used by the program are the composition of music and the scientific analysis of sound, creative writing, and information technology. In short, students enrolled in the program engage in inquiry related to music and sound; rhythms and pulses; harmonics and resonances; applied technology; and the physical, geometrical, and psycho-physical bases of sound, acoustics, and vibrating systems.

Assessment of student learning at Evergreen College is done by the faculty who team-teach each program and who employ narrative evaluations rather than letter grades. Students regularly discuss their progress one on one with faculty members and receive written progress evaluations. During this process, students are also invited to submit written evaluations of faculty. In addition, students prepare self-evaluations, in which they reflect on their accomplishments, learning environment, new understandings, and goals for the future. Finally, when nearing graduation, Evergreen students work with a faculty advisor to create a Summative Self-Evaluation, in which they reflect on their undergraduate experience, including progress toward their individual learning goals across their entire undergraduate career.

In short, the Evergreen State College is committed to interdisciplinary and highly collaborative inquiry-driven teaching and learning practices. By taking ownership in planning and reflecting on their learning, in concert with assessing their academic progress, Evergreen students learn by engaging in real problems and, in so doing, enhance their capacity to pursue ideas with imagination as well as discipline.

Worcester Polytechnic University

Massachusetts' Worcester Polytechnic Institute (WPI) was founded in 1865 with the motto Theory and Practice and with a mission to combine academic coursework and theory with practical experiences aimed at developing in students a deep appreciation of societal and global complexities. WPI seeks to prepare innovative leaders in technology, science, engineering, management, and the humanities by combining theory with practice and giving WPI students the opportunity to gain real-world experience, develop professional skills, work collaboratively, and accept challenges, no matter how complex, with confidence. All undergraduate students must complete four project requirements in order to earn their degree. These include (1) the Great Problems Seminars (GPS), (2) a Humanities and Arts Project, (3) the Interactive Qualifying Project, and (4) the Major Qualifying Project.

During their freshman year, students are required to enroll in two GPS courses, which serve as an introduction to university-level research and project work. These seminars are closely tied to current events, societal problems, and themes of current global importance. Beginning on their first day of classes, GPS freshmen immerse themselves in some of the world's most pressing concerns by addressing creating solutions for large-scale social and technical problems.

Recent examples of GPS seminars are the Grand Challenges and Heal the World Seminars. The Grand Challenges Seminar focused, thematically, on engineering and material science and involved a sequence of team and individual inquiry projects tied to the major challenges facing engineering in the twenty-first century, including energy, transportation, housing, food distribution, recycling, sustainability, and health care. The Heal the World Seminar began with the study of the biology of infectious disease and moved on to the management of disease control while assigning teams of three to five students to complete a major inquiry project accompanied by a public presentation of findings and proposed solutions.

During their sophomore year, WPI students complete their Humanities and Arts requirement in concert with WPI's other degree requirements and with a particular focus upon inquiry-based approaches to student learning. This requirement engages students in both theory and practice through (1) introducing students to the breadth, diversity, and creativity of human experience as expressed in the humanities and the arts; (2) enriching students' understanding of themselves; (3) encouraging students to reflect on their responsibilities to others in local, national, and global communities; (4) encouraging students to develop the ability to think critically and independently about the world; (5) enhancing students' ability to communicate effectively with others in a spirit of openness and cooperation; (6) deepening students' ability to apply concepts and skills in a focused thematic area through sustained critical inquiry; and (7) kindling in students a life-long interest in the humanities and the arts.

In order to qualify for graduation, during their junior and senior years students participate in the WPI Projects Program, through which they complete two significant projects under faculty supervision and in cooperation with public and private employers. These projects include the Interactive Qualifying Project (IQP) and the Major Qualifying Project (MQP). Since the beginning of WPI's projects requirement in 1972, thousands of student projects have been completed in cooperation with industry and with nonprofit and public organizations. The Projects Program offers employers the opportunity to join WPI in providing workplace experiences for future engineers, scientists, and business managers. Throughout the course of their project development, students are supervised and advised by a WPI faculty member while external sponsors also play a supportive advisory role. In order to earn a bachelor of science degree, students must submit two professional-level reports to their advisor and sponsor, and they are encouraged to make formal oral presentations at the sponsor's work site. Abstracts of all projects are published.

During their junior year, students must complete the IQP requirement. In teams of two to four, and under the direct guidance of one or more faculty advisors, students address problems in which science or technology intersect with social challenges and human needs. This interdisciplinary requirement helps WPI graduates to understand, as citizens and as professionals, how their careers will affect the larger society.

While many IQP ideas come from external sponsors, others are proposed by faculty members or by students themselves. In brief, an IQP involves at least one unit of academic work, which is the equivalent of three courses, and it can be competed in a single term or spread over multiple terms. The IQP is an intentionally broad and integrative experience. Student teams are drawn from across disciplines, the project is not typically related to students' major fields, and the methods used by IQP students are sometimes taken from training in the social sciences or humanities.

Although many IQPs are completed in proximity to WPI, approximately 60 percent are completed through WPI's Global Perspective Program at one of WPI's project centers in Africa, the Americas, Asia, Australia, or Europe. More than 5,000 students have completed off-campus projects at more than 25 project centers on five continents since the program's inception in the 1980s. WPI projects have had a positive impact on individuals, organizations, and agencies around the globe. In Venice, for example, students helped reduce damage to canal walls and cataloged the city's endangered public art, and in Thailand, WPI students brought solar energy to remote tribes and assessed environmental threats facing residents of the Klong Toey slum.

During their senior year, students complete a Major Qualifying Project (MQP), which provides them the opportunity to gain high-level design or engrossing research experience within their major field. Generally undertaken in teams and often sponsored by corporations or other external organizations, this capstone project is an integral element of WPI's project-enriched education and serves as a springboard to professional careers, graduate school, and rewarding personal and public lives. Each spring, student teams representing all of WPI's academic departments present their major projects to faculty advisors, external sponsors, and the public in an annual exhibition of exemplary student projects.[5]

George Mason University, New Century College

George Mason University (GMU), with its three satellite campuses, is the largest public university in Virginia.[6] In 1995, GMU launched the New Century College (NCC) as a small, independent, experimental college within the institution; it was intended to create and house innovative degree programs and learning environments to prepare students for the emerging global economy. One hallmark of NCC faculty is a commitment to continuously explore new teaching and learning approaches, new academic and community partnerships, and new curricular structures—and, in so doing, to challenge traditional educational models.

The NCC curriculum is based upon several innovative programs that were originally created and nurtured by a handful of GMU faculty members who sought to change both the learning environment and learning outcomes for students. These innovations included "writing across the curriculum," in which writing is infused into all disciplines across the undergraduate curriculum. Two other programs, spearheaded by the Office of Instructional Development, promote the widespread use of technology, as well as numerous comprehensive theme-based learning communities, which are based on experiential themes such as service learning, community-based research, community action, internships, and advocacy.

Coursework for all undergraduate students is organized around nine core competencies: communication, critical thinking, information technology, problem-solving, valuing, aesthetic response, social interaction, effective citizenship, and creating global perspectives. As these core competencies suggest, the mission of NCC is anchored in the proposition that a meaningful undergraduate education requires far more than the acquisition of knowledge. Students are expected to demonstrate their growing mastery in each of the nine core competencies throughout the course of their studies through assignments, projects, reflection, self-assessment, and the creation of semester-end and graduation portfolios.

Students at NCC pursue a bachelor's degree in Integrative Studies. The hallmarks of NCC's Integrative Studies curriculum are reflected in three graduation requirements: participation in a learning community, experiential learning, and the senior capstone.

NCC's learning communities are theme-based and interdisciplinary, not course-based, with each theme focused on tackling complex problems from multiple academic disciplines and taught by teams of faculty from these different disciplines. Because most courses emphasize collaborative and experiential learning, most instructors require end-of-term essays or portfolios to ensure that students comprehend knowledge, can effectively communicate ideas, and are developing their critical thinking skills. NCC students also have the option of participating in Living and Learning Communities (LLC) by living in the same residence hall as the classmates in their LLC. These students are at once challenged and supported by faculty, academic advisors, and residence hall support staff as they develop their communication, critical thinking, and leadership skills. Experiential learning—the development of connections between theoretical, classroom-based knowledge and real-world settings—is another requirement at NCC. Students must participate in study-abroad programs, service learning, internships, and cooperative programs with public and private sector employers. While immersed in the field, NCC students enhance their capacity to effectively communicate their ideas in writing and through oral presentations and gain diverse perspectives that can contribute to their future involvement as citizens in our democracy.

NCC students must also enroll in a Senior Capstone Synthesis, which requires students to reflect upon, analyze, and evaluate their

college experiences in both written documents and oral presentations. Each student eventually publishes his or her personal reflections in a final graduation portfolio, which is evaluated by a faculty
member and made available to prospective employers and admissions committees at graduate schools.

In summary, the mission, goals, teaching methods, and assessment
practices at New Century College exemplify inquiry-driven learning
in action. Given the urgent need for interdisciplinary and integrative
approaches to learning in today's work environment, NCC's Integrative Studies degree incorporates the practical application of knowledge
with credit-earning internships, opportunities to study abroad, and
service-learning experiences to help students connect and make sense
of increasingly disparate knowledge to address complex problems
within a global society.

The Inquiry-Guided Learning Initiative
at North Carolina State University

In 1996, the faculty at North Carolina State University (NC State) initiated an effort to redesign the undergraduate curriculum to engage
students in "inquiry-guided learning" (IGL). The focus on IGL began
after a graduate student suggested that, although the university emphasized the importance of critical thinking, relatively few faculty
members gave students explicit guidance in how to think critically.
Working together, the student and a small faculty committee submit-
ted a grant proposal to the Hewlett Foundation seeking funding to
improve the general education curriculum. Under the banner of IGL,
the proposal emphasized general education courses as the place to
empower students to take responsibility for their own learning and
provide training in critical thinking. The proposal emphasized
a continuum of inquiry from freshman general education courses all
the way to capstone experiences in the major.

The Hewlett Foundation funded the initial proposal and awarded
two successive grants to NC State's inquiry-guided learning initiative.
Programmatic implementation of the IGL initiative included (1)
a First-Year Inquiry Program, which reached approximately one-third

of incoming freshmen; (2) a First-Year Seminar Program in the College of Humanities and Social Sciences; (3) selected courses throughout the undergraduate program, both in general education and the major; and (4) nine departments from the university's ten colleges, which introduced inquiry-guided learning into a sequence of courses in the major. Between 1996 and 2004, more than 200 faculty and more than 60 academic and administrative units on campus designed IGL courses to facilitate inquiry-guided learning for 6,000 students. The program promoted four broad student-learning outcomes: critical thinking, developing habits of independent inquiry, responsibility for one's own learning, and intellectual growth and development. A shared commitment to these outcomes aligned the IGL initiative with writing and speaking across the curriculum, undergraduate academic program review, and assessment—three other major emphases on campus.

The climate created by the IGL initiative encouraged innovation by supporting faculty who transformed their courses into inquiry-guided learning experiences. Administrative support generally included campus-wide symposia on inquiry-guided learning, in-house workshops on inquiry-guided learning and assessment, individual consultations, peer observation of teaching, opportunities for faculty to participate in conferences and national projects, and financial support for wider dissemination of IGL. Faculty who developed, assessed, and implemented the IGL initiative believe that integration of inquiry-guided learning across general education and the majors would never have been possible had it been based on a single model of inquiry-guided learning or a prescribed set of approaches. They reasoned that in a large research university, success would best be achieved by focusing on broad student learning outcomes coupled with a flexible, shared understanding of the principles of inquiry-guided learning. Because participating faculty translated outcomes into terms that made sense within their respective fields of study, such flexibility facilitated the integration of inquiry-guided learning into general education courses as well as courses in the major and, in turn, opened the way for inquiry-guided learning across the entire undergraduate curriculum.

University of Wisconsin–Madison: Three Pockets of Innovation

The Evergreen State College, Worcester Polytechnic Institute, and New Century College all developed innovative undergraduate programs of study that would likely be difficult, if not impossible, to set up at many long-established colleges and universities. Nonetheless, we identified several pockets of innovation from the University of Wisconsin–Madison, one of the nation's major land-grant universities. In recent years, faculty and staff at the university have pursued three approaches variously aimed at developing what we refer to as "inquiry-driven learners": (1) First-Year Interest Groups, (2) the University of Wisconsin Teaching Academy and its fellows, and (3) Student Innovation Initiatives.

FIRST-YEAR INTEREST GROUPS

In 2001, the University of Wisconsin–Madison initiated a pilot program entitled First-Year Interest Groups, or FIGs. The mission of the FIG program is to enhance freshman learning through the development of small communities of students, faculty, and staff that foster academic and social connections to support diversity education, contribute to general education goals and learning, contribute to the development of living and learning communities, and offer opportunities for integrated and interdisciplinary learning across multiple academic disciplines. Each FIG consists of an independent "learning community" of about 20 students who enroll together in a cluster of three classes. A primary seminar course is limited to those 20 students and is led by a single faculty member, who has chosen a substantive theme that is integrated into the other two courses in which students are enrolled. The other two courses, chosen for relevance to the FIG theme, are most often large-lecture or gateway courses on campus.[7] The integration of courses across multiple diverse academic disciplines aims to encourage discovery and exploration of the ways in which these disciplines are interrelated, thereby enhancing students' capacities to apply divergent modes of inquiry and approaches to problem-solving.

Faculty members who teach FIG seminar courses are responsible for integrating relevant content from the cluster's other two linked courses. They identify appropriate potential linking courses and then work with FIG program administrators, who secure enrollment slots from academic departments. Almost all courses linked within a FIG meet either general education requirements or breadth requirements within general majors, and all FIG faculty members are encouraged to collaborate with their linked faculty to optimally integrate content from their courses into the main seminar. Such collaboration often begins by simply sharing syllabi, but it can move to the use of complementary readings and activities or sequencing course content for a more effective chronological presentation.

The goal is to create an intentionally interdisciplinary experience that constitutes at least two-thirds of each student's academic schedules. As a result, students are not simply sitting in classes together but rather are immersed in a shared intellectual learning environment that challenges them to advance their capacities to utilize diverse ways of knowing. FIG professors use a range of pedagogical approaches to integrate cross-disciplinary course content and encourage students to engage their developing critical thinking skills. Moreover, assessments in these courses ask students to identify and evaluate the interrelations between disciplines while framing personal questions to guide their inquiry.

Three examples of FIG course clusters are (a) Seeing the Forest for the Trees through Sustainable Use, which clusters courses on forest and wildlife ecology with general botany, and a geography course on populations and resource use; (b) China and the Environment, a FIG cluster that connects a history course on China's environmental policies with a first-semester Chinese language course, and an environmental studies course taught from the humanist perspective; and (c) Race, Ethnicity, and Inequality in American Education, a FIG cluster that connects an education policy studies course of the same name with a sociology course on problems facing American ethnic and racial minorities and an educational psychology course on adolescent development.

The FIGs model also offers curricular, extracurricular, and other structural advantages that enhance students' ability to connect socially and academically within the university. FIG students frequently, and spontaneously, create course-independent study groups that lead to inquiry, collaboration, and challenging dialogue as they collaboratively share their insights and ideas. Some FIGs also include service-learning opportunities, extending the out-of-class experiences as students engage in service throughout their local community. Frequent out-of-class activities are facilitated by faculty affiliated with a respective FIG group, and this blurring of social and academic roles often leads to a shared sense of inquiry between students and faculty alike.

Assessment by university administrators of the FIG program, which began in 2001 and continues through the present, indicates that students participating in the program experience the following outcomes: higher college retention rates; enhanced abilities to identify relationships among academic disciplines; higher levels of integration of course information; more formal and informal interaction with faculty in and out of the classroom; higher levels of interaction with peers; and greater gains in communication skills. Moreover, the GPAs for each FIG cohort have been significantly higher than the GPAs of peer groups, even though their academic profiles—including average ACT scores and average class rank—have, on average, been lower. Not insignificantly, faculty members who have taught FIG courses often comment on the high levels of student engagement and participation in class, and they frequently remark on the fact that their FIGs students rarely miss class.

The FIG program has continued to grow over the past decade. Whereas 75 students enrolled in four pilot FIGs in 2001, beginning in 2011 as many as 1,200 out of 6,000 first-year students have the option of taking a FIG. Although the program originated in the College of Letters and Science, by the fall of 2010 all schools and colleges offering undergraduate majors at the University of Wisconsin–Madison participated in the First-Year Interest Groups.

THE UNIVERSITY OF WISCONSIN–MADISON TEACHING ACADEMY

With a focus on providing innovative teaching resources to instructors, the Teaching Academy of the University of Wisconsin–Madison (UWTA) was established in 1993 by the Faculty Senate.[8] The mission of the UWTA is to promote effective teaching and learning both on campus and nationally by encouraging innovation, experimentation, and dialogue among faculty, instructional staff, and future teachers. The UWTA has six core functions: providing a forum for dialogue on effective teaching and learning; communicating the best practices of teaching and learning; linking individuals interested in improving the teaching and learning process; sponsoring professional development events; analyzing issues and making recommendations on university policies affecting teaching and learning; and creating a learning community for sharing teaching and learning resources.

Outstanding educators who are invested in their teaching and are committed to enriching the learning environment for students are nominated by their peers to become UWTA fellows. UWTA particularly welcomes scholars who have demonstrated excellence through classroom innovation, program development, grant funding, publications, presentations, or committee work related to teaching and learning. Several of the UWTA's fellows have been recognized for their teaching, not only at the University of Wisconsin–Madison, but also on a national level. For example, in 2009 WTA fellow Professor Teri Balser, who has since been named dean of the College of Agriculture and Life Sciences at the University of Florida, was named United States Professor of the Year for doctoral and research universities by the Council for the Advancement and Support of Education (CASE) and the Carnegie Foundation for the Advancement of Teaching. This honor is bestowed annually on only four professors from across the nation.

Professor Balser's specialty has been engaging students in inquiry across the full spectrum of learning environments, from large lecture halls filled with hundreds of undergraduates enrolled in introductory environmental studies classes for nonscience majors to seminars for graduate students. Well-known for her work promoting inquiry as a lived experience, she employs innovative approaches to inquiry. Balser places herself in the role of the learner by consistently soliciting feedback from students so as to best match her teaching with their respective learning styles, and creatively using information technology in the classroom to interact with her students. She strives to create an optimal learning environment in which students continuously challenge themselves, and each other, by asking tough questions, initiating collaborative discussions, engaging in creative inquiry, and reflecting deeply upon the subject matter of the course and its application outside of class to contemporary social problems.

The UWTA provides resources to fellows such as Teri Balser in ways that enable them to develop innovative teaching methods aimed at enhancing student learning. And even though UWTA fellows are spread across colleges and schools at one of the largest research universities in the world, they are reshaping the undergraduate experience one classroom at a time for thousands of students, encouraging and supporting them to pursue new ideas with a full measure of creativity, enthusiasm, innovation, and rigor.

STUDENT INITIATIVES

Each year, the University of Wisconsin–Madison Technology Enterprise Cooperative (UW-TEC) spearheads three major innovation initiatives for all undergraduate students on campus.[9] UW-TEC, created in 1992 and cosponsored by the College of Engineering, School of Business, and College of Agricultural and Life Sciences, has a campus-wide mission: to stimulate creativity and invention within students, to create student awareness of entrepreneurial opportunities, and to foster partnerships between students, faculty, and business leaders that give students hands-on experience exploring and pursuing unique high-technology start-up business opportunities.

One of UW-TEC's unique roles is to give students hands-on experience creating new technology-based businesses. Accordingly, UW-TEC annually sponsors three initiatives, all of which provide opportunities for the entrepreneurial sectors of the business community to participate with students, faculty, and staff in a wide range of educational, outreach, and technology business-development activities.

- Seminars and classes that are held throughout the academic year for students feature guest speakers and focus upon innovation, creativity, technology entrepreneurialism, and how to start a business.

- The G. Steven Burrill Technology Business Plan Competition is an annual competition in which teams of students select a technology-based business idea and develop a business plan. Finalists are chosen by a panel of judges from the business community and students can win cash prizes of up to $10,000.
- The Schoofs Prize for Creativity and Innovation Days event is an annual competition for UW-Madison undergraduates to stimulate creativity and invention.

UW-TEC's annual creativity competition and its sponsorship of Innovation Days provide a compelling version of innovation in action, one that is grounded in inquiry and the power of a good idea. Each year, this competition draws dozens of innovative, entrepreneurial students who, while competing for cash prizes, receive critical feedback from university and business leaders, support to bring their ideas to fruition, the opportunity to develop a prototype in university engineering labs, assistance in filing patents for their ideas, and help in establishing a business based upon their ideas.

Past winning designs include: (1) mechanical engineering senior Tom Gerold's MicroMag Stent Deployment System, an invention that allows surgeons to use electronic systems for implanting stents within the diseased arteries of patients; (2) a breast milk filter for mothers diagnosed with HIV-1, which binds HIV-1proteins and removes them from the milk, but retains other nutrients; and (3) the Lace Master, a machine that enables an injured or disabled people to tie their shoes tightly with just one hand.

A second student initiative at the University of Wisconsin–Madison is the Wiscontrepreneur Initiative. In 2007, the Ewing Marion Kauffman Foundation awarded UW-Madison a major grant to support entrepreneurial activities throughout the undergraduate curriculum as well as promote new business entities and socially beneficial organizations. The mission of the initiative is based on the premise that entrepreneurship is a critical component of growing Wisconsin's economy and creating high-tech, high-wage fields. Accordingly, the Wiscontrepreneur Initiative seeks to inspire the spirit and skills of entrepreneurial studies in all academic fields, especially in the arts, the humanities, and in service learning.[10]

Activities sponsored by the Wiscontrepreneur Initiative include (1) seven academic courses offered by colleges, schools, and departments of the university, including the School of Human Ecology, the Biomedical Engineering Department, and the business and law schools; (2) an entrepreneurial residential learning community, which is housed in one of the residence halls and affords undergraduate students the opportunity to enroll in courses focused on entrepreneurialism; (3) the MERLIN Venture Mentoring Service, which pairs new business owners with seasoned business professionals who serve as mentors; and (4) an annual student innovation competition entitled the "100-Hour Challenge."

The Wiscontrepreneur 100-Hour Challenge challenges students to engage in inquiry and innovative thinking by creating innovative products or services using materials from the University of Wisconsin Surplus with a Purpose (SWAP) Program, a campus unit that sells surplus university supplies, ranging from lab equipment to athletic gear to electronics. As part of the challenge, students are given a voucher that allows them to purchase raw materials worth $15 or less. Students have 100 hours to innovate using their own ideas and the SWAP items. During this time period, they must report to a panel of judges, communicate their work through such means as digital photo sets, videos, or other electronic communications that are posted on a publicly accessible website. Contestants work on their entries at a university workspace equipped with hardware, software, electronics, as well as art, sewing, pottery, glass, and metalwork supplies. In accepting this challenge, students are encouraged to "Remember, entrepreneurship has three parts: having an idea, taking action, and creating value. To succeed in this Challenge, test assumptions, seize opportunities, and be creative."[11]

Students compete for cash prizes in categories including Most Creative, Most Value Generated, and Most Social Value Generated, and one student wins the People's Choice Award. Past winners include the Dorm Disposer, a small worm composter that sits on a windowsill or desk and receives discarded food, which is then consumed by worms. The student inventors began their inquiry with the realization that each of the 40,000 students at the university casts off up to 1,500 pounds of waste each year, totaling roughly 60 million pounds. Thus, they invented a way to reduce food waste.

Collaborative Undergraduate Research and Inquiry: St. Olaf College

In 2010, Minnesota's St. Olaf College began offering undergraduate students the opportunity to participate in collaborative research projects with faculty members in a program called the Collaborative Undergraduate Research and Inquiry (CURI).[12] CURI is a campus-wide initiative that seeks to provide as many students as possible with inquiry-driven research opportunities to explore and pursue inquiry as well as to work collaboratively with faculty in choosing research topics and framing research questions. The program facilitates collaborative research among teams of faculty and students in the natural sciences and mathematics and in the fine arts, humanities, social sciences, and interdisciplinary and general studies. The CURI program was founded on the belief that inquiry takes many different forms, that there is much more to learning than just what happens in classrooms, and perhaps most importantly, that existing methods need to be applied in novel settings in order to advance human knowledge.

CURI projects take place every summer, when students receive accommodations in college residence halls for eight weeks and commit to 40 hours a week of hands-on collaborative research and inquiry with faculty. Participants work with faculty to collectively frame research questions, access extant knowledge, and interpret and synthesize research findings. Students participate in weekly research conferences to engage in dialogue regarding the previous week's research, recursively shape their research questions, and then develop research agendas for the coming week. All participants communicate their research findings at a symposium in which they must respond to the questions of attendees and prepare posters and papers for public display.

Examples of student/faculty inquiry-based research include (a) "The United States 2008 Financial Crisis and Its Lessons for China," (b) "Computing the Dynamics of Political Blogs," and (c) "A Large-Scale Approach to Computational Linguistics." In the first example, a faculty participant of Chinese nationality paired with an undergraduate student to explore ways in which the United States revised its governance of the financial sector in the aftermath of the 2008 financial crisis, with a special focus on China's rising status in the world economy. The computing dynamics project paired a political science and information technology professor with undergraduate students who used computers to manage and process large volumes of heterogeneous data to explore the relationship between Internet media sources and voter attitudes. Finally, the computational linguistics project represented an interdisciplinary effort to bring high-performance computing techniques to the study of computational linguistics to facilitate cross-disciplinary research. In the near future St. Olaf plans to expand CURI research opportunities by incorporating them across the entire undergraduate curriculum.

Freshman Learning Project: Indiana University Bloomington

The Freshman Learning Project (FLP) at Indiana University Bloomington is a programmatic innovation that provides support for faculty members seeking to develop new teaching methods that stimulate inquiry and enhance student learning.[13] While the FLP serves faculty members who teach courses across the entire undergraduate curriculum, the project has a particular focus on the large introductory and gateway courses that are frequently required of freshmen students. Since it began in 1998, the FLP has enrolled an annual cohort of about 12 peer-nominated faculty fellows from multiple academic disciplines who participate in an intensive two-week summer training session that explores innovative approaches to student inquiry and learning, addressing challenges faced by students in their introductory classes, new ways of helping students overcome learning obstacles, and setting high expectations for student performance.

During the training session, fellows read articles by scholars of teaching and learning and then, during daily sessions, are encouraged to challenge themselves and their colleagues to question this extant knowledge and consider nontraditional approaches to teaching and learning. To cultivate student learning across disciplines, fellows follow a seven-step model:[14]

1. *Define a bottleneck skill.* Fellows identify a skill in their course that many students find difficult to master. For example, freshman English students may have difficulty composing a thesis statement.

2. *Define the basic learning tasks.* Fellows guide students as they define and explore the steps that experts execute to perform the bottleneck skill. As they work with the instructor to identify and define the attributes of the skill, students develop a commitment to working toward mastery.

3. *Model the bottleneck skill.* After instructors model completion of the skill or task for the students, they analyze the modeling together and determine whether it synthesized all the essential attributes of the skill.

4. *Create occasions for students to practice the steps and receive feedback.* Fellows construct assignments, team activities, and other learning exercises to give students the opportunity to perform each of the skills or tasks they have modeled. As students complete these exercises, fellows provide feedback aimed at facilitating students' mastery of these skills.

5. *Motivate students to excel.* During the planning process, fellows develop the approaches they will utilize to create a positive learning environment in which students can achieve a series of successes that help develop a drive to succeed.

6. *Assess how well students are mastering the learning tasks.* Fellows create new, alternate, and appropriate forms of assessment for providing formative feedback to their students.

Once familiar with the model, fellows use it to design summer courses, observe fellow teachers, and continue to refine their pedagogy in sessions with their peers. Beyond the two-week session, FLP staff continue to work with fellows as they implement and recursively develop new ideas for teaching and learning. Moreover, faculty in this program commit to engage the greater academic community by sharing their ideas through symposia, newsletter articles, department meetings, informal presentations, and dialogue with colleagues.

University of New Mexico College of Nursing, Critical Thinking Skills Resource

The Critical Thinking Skills (CTS) web resource at the University of New Mexico (UNM) School of Nursing provides a virtual community intended primarily for nursing students, faculty, and staff who seek to enhance their understanding of critical thinking and the development of cognitive skills.[15] The CTS resource nests links to refereed journal articles, department meetings, white papers, and news articles in an online discussion forum for sharing insights and information. The CTS resource was developed by two faculty members—Patsy Duphorne and Jean Giddens—to identify resources across academic disciplines that promote the use of critical thinking among faculty and students in a variety of settings, especially health care.

To support a community of practice engaged in developing the capacities of students to think critically, Professors Duphorne and Giddens encourage site users to reflect upon the following questions: (1) Who do I know that is a critical thinker, and what characteristics or traits would describe this person? (2) What does critical thinking mean to me, and how does it differ from "normal" thinking? (3) When do I use critical thinking—do I use it in writing papers, taking exams, reading assignments, doing presentations, practicing skills, caring for patients? and (4) How can I assess my thinking skills and improve them? By placing critical thinking resources in a freely available global forum, these two professors have shown that developing inquiry-driven learners need not be costly. Rather, by setting forth key questions, a rich set of resources, and a free, open, and global forum, two individuals can make a world of difference.

Institutional Practices for Educating Inquiry-Driven Learners

There is a range of practices that cuts across the models presented above and other like-minded initiatives that we have studied. We have identified three clusters of such practices that can be used to cultivate inquiry-driven learners: (1) the teaching and learning that occurs in classroom discussions, online interactions, and research endeavors; (2) the structure of courses; and (3) missions, policies, and strategic planning.

Teaching and Learning in the Classroom, Online Interactions, and Research Activities

Within any classroom setting—a lecture hall, a seminar, an online course, a research lab—professors have the opportunity to develop the major capacities of an inquiry-driven learner in their students. The capacity to frame meaningful questions is especially important, for many of the most formidable challenges and opportunities that students will address in their personal, public, and professional lives have not yet been identified. Thus, rather than organizing classes mostly around content acquisition, faculty can work closely with students to inspire and enhance their capacity to frame questions that matter and to guide their inquiry. Such a shift frees students from being held hostage by extant literature and questions that others have sought to answer, and it inoculates them against faculty control of the dominant discourse. Inquiry-driven classes also press learners to modify their burning questions throughout the course of their inquiry and to recalibrate or change their burning questions in response to new data, information, and occurrences as they arise.

Worcester Polytechnic Institute (WPI) provides an example of how to teach the framing of burning questions. In WPI's Great Problems Seminars, students work to identify the great questions facing human societies across the globe, then participate in a process of collaborative inquiry with peers and faculty to question, research, and analyze potential answers. By focusing on great questions facing humanity in the modern era, WPI helps students frame questions that can facilitate their development as inquiry-driven learners. And regardless of format, collaboration encourages and supports students as they blend and reconcile their own ideas, values, and perspectives with those of peers and instructors. It invites students to engage in spirited dialogue among themselves and supports problem-solving activities with their peers and instructors.

In addition to framing meaningful questions, professors can provide students with opportunities to appreciate the importance of engaging in independent and critical thought by encouraging them to sift through diverse sources of knowledge and information. In this way, inquiry-driven learners learn how to prioritize and synthesize information in the search for promising ideas.

This is crucial because the traditional means of accessing news, information, and even music—such as television network and radio shows—are increasingly becoming irrelevant. In their place, Internet-driven sources of online news services, information and music, which are often paired with social networking sites, are changing the nature of human communication. One provocative aspect of these Internet-based technologies is that users are able not only to select their preferred sources of news, information, and music but also to create exclusive social networks, or circle of friends, to which they wish to belong. As a result, an entire generation of students is easily able to stratify their social experience, routinely "opting in" to specialized sources of information and genres of music, using sites such as the Drudge Report, Twitter, and Pandora. As a result, the lives and perspectives of students can become narrower, and these students run the risk of encountering fewer and fewer opposing viewpoints, experiencing fewer genres of art and music, and building fewer meaningful relationships with people from diverse backgrounds, perspectives, and personal histories.

In response to this modern reality, undergraduate students need an education that obliges them to become independent thinkers who purposefully consider, rather than immediately react to, the constant flow of information. They need guided practice in seeking out and engaging diverse sources information and communities of inquiry.

Inquiry-driven colleges and universities need to provide students with a wide range of experiences aimed at enhancing their capacity to discriminate among these diverse sources as they continue to evolve.

The twenty-first century workplace is one in which communication and problem-solving across professional fields and communities—including the Internet—is the currency. It is, therefore, imperative to provide students with sufficient training in divergent modes of inquiry so that they can effectively move between problem spaces and communities. This need not necessitate a veritable overhaul of long-standing classroom practices. For example, classroom instructors can learn from the approaches of those outside their home academic and professional field to analyze and solve problems, and by bringing their own inquiry practices into their teaching, they can guide students toward a fuller appreciation of the importance of developing expertise in divergent modes of inquiry in their problem-solving. Similarly, by bringing in guest speakers with varying academic and professional perspectives, an instructor can give students the opportunity to experience new ways of thinking, analysis, and problem-solving through interactions with these guests. Finally, experiential learning opportunities, such as community service projects and professional internships, also help students strengthen their knowledge, understanding, and application of divergent modes of inquiry in cultivating ideas.

For example, in the First-Year Interest Groups (FIGs) program at the University of Wisconsin–Madison, some students take a course on community organizing and coalition building while simultaneously participating in service-learning placements in the community, working with groups as diverse as seniors in retirement communities and individuals about to be released from prison. In working in both a traditional academic setting and in a field placement with people of diverse backgrounds, students learn to compare disciplinary approaches to framing questions for solving problems, explore interrelations among approaches, and reflect on how these approaches can be brought to bear in addressing real-world problems. In sum, participating students enhance their capacity to apply divergent approaches to problem-solving, as well as their ability to pursue inquiry as a dynamic and recursive experience together with their peers, instructors, and members of the extended community.

Structure of Courses

For the most part, academic courses across the higher learning are viewed as units of knowledge to be transferred from professors to students. As a result, courses are structured around substantive bodies of knowledge, majors, and assessment of students' acquisition of this knowledge. In order to develop inquiry-driven learners, the emphasis of this conventional course structure requires redirection, namely, from straightforward knowledge acquisition to critically analyzing extant knowledge and, in turn, using this knowledge to frame and solve real-world problems.

Existing coursework runs the gamut, from conducting independent research and writing papers, to developing presentations and participating in group projects. Building on such activities, as students read and engage in research they can be encouraged by their instructors to engage in ongoing dialogue with the authors of the materials they are assigned to read for class. In particular, students can view inquiry into existing knowledge as inextricably linked to critical thought, and thus they can learn both to engage the information upon the page and also to critically analyze its relationship to solving real problems. In simple terms, students' reading and research ought not simply to consist of a writer-driven exercise in compliance. Rather than resigning their intellectual agency over to the mere absorption of existing sources of knowledge and information, inquiry-driven learners engage in ongoing dialogue and actively challenge the subject matter they encounter. In short, it is important to emphasize that students must be taught not to simply absorb, accept, and regurgitate information, but rather to internalize it through deep reflection. Creating "sacred spaces" for contemplation is not to be underestimated.

An example of student research is the Collaborative Undergraduate Research and Inquiry Program at St. Olaf College described earlier in this chapter. Courses in this program are structured so as to engage students in independent study and research that emphasizes using inquiry questions as the starting point for conducting research and for engaging sources of information. The program also affords students the opportunity to develop twenty-first-century skills, such as collaboration with peers and faculty members and conducting public presentations using contemporary tools of technology.

Finally, traditional undergraduate coursework can give students the ability to express and communicate their ideas. Worcester Polytechnic Institute (WPI) provides an example of how to enrich and enlarge undergraduate training by sequencing courses and assignments in ways that help students to express and communicate their ideas. In order to graduate, students must be able to express their ideas in writing and through speech via a Major Qualifying Project (MQP). This project enables students to gain valuable experience in their major field through a capstone project, and it prepares them for professional careers, graduate school, and their public lives. These MQP projects, which are undertaken in teams often sponsored by corporations or other external organizations, afford students an additional opportunity for collaboration and problem-solving.

Mission Statements, Policies, and Strategic Planning

Finally, we wish to emphasize that college and university mission statements, policies, and strategic planning processes ought to emphasize all aspects of becoming an inquiry-driven learner. Not least among these, we would place particular emphasis on the pursuit of ideas that contribute to the common good. The contemporary world puts constant pressure on our colleges and universities to embrace privatization—often at the expense of the common good—by relying on business models that target resources toward generating economic gain. But if we do not encourage our students to serve the common good, we fail to teach them how to care for themselves as well. For by caring for society and the environment, especially in an interconnected, global, and overpopulated world, students ultimately care for themselves. Genuine caring for humanity and the environment, especially in an increasingly interconnected, global, and overpopulated world, should be placed at the forefront of developing inquiry-driven learners and reflected in institutional missions, policies, and strategic planning processes.

A Concluding Note

The initiatives taken by faculty, administrators, and staff that are highlighted in this chapter all embody a commitment to cultivate within students many of the capabilities that constitute our concept of the inquiry-driven learner. Rather than placing primary emphasis on the competitiveness, résumé-building, and self-branding that has captured the imagination of many students and faculty, these and other like-minded initiatives hold great promise to help bring students, faculty, and staff together in the pursuit of inquiry, creativity, and innovation. As we consider these initiatives, we see transformations with respect to teaching and learning. These initiatives and the practices that accompany them present a challenge to the status quo and also to strategies for doing "business" differently. Building on such initiatives, we invite individuals across the higher learning—from faculty and administrators to students and staff—to join us in continuing an ongoing search for ideas for strengthening in our students the capacity to pursue ideas with discipline and imagination.

Chapter 1 · *Contemporary Discourse on the Purpose of a College Education*

1. Bernard Murchland (1976) used the phrase "eclipse of liberal education."

2. Lewis and many others enthusiastically embrace what Bobby Fong (2004) refers to as "the formation of character for citizenship and service to society" (p. 10)—a longstanding pillar of liberal and general education in this country.

3. In 1992 the National Endowment for the Humanities published a monograph entitled *Telling the Truth,* which argued that the aim of education should be "truth-telling: the effort to discover the truth" (Cheney, 1992, p. 6).

4. To be sure, various individuals and associations take exception to our proposition that there is no widely shared view about the purpose of a college education. For example, Terry Rhodes published an article anchored to the proposition that there is widespread agreement on the outcomes of a general (college) education. In his words: "Faculty across the country continue to report that their students need a strong knowledge base to achieve success in today's global society. The set of *essential learning outcomes* identified by faculty encompasses not only basic intellectual and practical abilities (such as written, oral, and graphical communication; critical thinking; problem-solving; quantitative literacy; and so on) but also individual and personal responsibility outcomes (such as ethical reasoning, intercultural understanding, and working with diverse others), as well as the ability to integrate one's learning across academic boundaries and apply knowledge in unscripted, complex situations" (2010, p. 14).

5. Observers of higher education have long suggested that many of the proposed purposes of a college education encompass an eclectic and unsettlingly amorphous list of desired outcomes—a trend long recognized in the literature on liberal education (Conrad & Wyer, 1980), general education

(Boyer & Levine, 1981), and undergraduate education in general (Conrad, 1978).

6. A notable exception has been the Association of American Colleges and Universities, as reflected in its 2007 report entitled *College Learning for the New Global Century.* A recent report by the Lumina Foundation for Education, "The Degree Qualifications Profile," proposed learning outcomes at the associate, bachelor's, and master's levels. Albeit a preliminary proposal, some of the learning outcomes proposed were clearly responsive to the world we live in (Lumina Foundation for Education, 2011).

7. As Conrad and Pratt (1981, p. 175) proposed, a comprehensive and holistic view of human development in college suggests that there be no separation of cognitive and affective, liberal and vocational, practical and theoretical. And in *A New Agenda for Higher Education,* William Sullivan and Matthew Rosin elaborate on the interdependence of liberal education and professional training and suggest bringing them together in advancing the concept of "practical reason" (2008, p. 93). Bruce Kimball (1995) argued that pragmatism (usefulness) has already influenced liberal education as embodied in the undergraduate curriculum.

Chapter 2 · A Rapidly Changing World and the Need for a Response

1. Disturbingly for many, the entire for-profit industry is heavily subsidized by federal tax dollars, with most for-profit institutions deriving almost all their revenue from federal student aid programs. For example, in 2009, the five largest for-profit institutions received 77% of their revenue from federal student aid programs, including Pell grants, Stafford loans, and PLUS loans, and this figure does not include revenue received from federal student loans that have been exempted by law, nor does it include revenue from Veterans' education benefits, federal job training programs, or State student financial aid programs (U.S. Department of Education, 2010, p. 43618). Concurrently, students at for-profit institutions take on more debt than students at nonprofit colleges and universities. In 2009, students at for-profit institutions borrowed 93% of their college costs compared to 49% at nonprofit institutions (ibid., 2009). Compounding this fact, students who attended for-profit institutions constituted 44% of the borrowers who defaulted on student loans in 2009, even though they represented only 7% of the total number of borrowers during that period (ibid., 2010, p. 43618).

Chapter 3 · Hurtling toward Obsolescence: The Default Purpose of a College Education

1. While we emphasize the influence of the 1945 *General Education in a Free Society: Report of the Harvard Committee,* for more than 25 centuries knowledge acquisition has been placed at the center of most writings regarding what it means to be an educated person. In recent years, one of the most prominent defenders of this position has been Paul Hirst (1974). Along with R. S. Peters, Hirst argues that the essence of being an educated person is to have both breadth and depth of knowledge (Hirst & Peters, 1970).

Chapter 4 · Portrayal of an Inquiry-Driven Learner

1. When we initially coined the term *inquiry-driven learner,* neither of us had ever come across the phrase. After conducting a search, we found that it has occasionally been used in K–16 settings. For example, Booker T. Washington High School for Engineering Professions in Houston, Texas, prepares students to be "inquiry-driven learners," and the School of Education and Human Development at Shenandoah University expects students to be "inquiry-driven." Notwithstanding these usages, along with occasional references to pedagogical approaches in the sciences aimed at preparing inquiry-driven learners, we have not found a definition of an inquiry-driven learner in the literature that resembles our definition.

2. To be sure, as Bruce Kimball (1986) elaborated on in *Orators and Philosophers: A History of the Idea of Liberal Education,* the idea of liberal education as the "continuing, ever-critical search for truth" (p. 11) is anchored in a philosophical tradition that reaches from Socrates and Plato and Aristotle to the present. Yet, as Kimball acknowledges (albeit indirectly), arresting ambiguity has surrounded the concept of liberal education since the fourth century BC. In Kimball's words: "Its glory is the freedom of the intellect; *its puzzle, as an educational philosophy* (our italics), is what else to teach besides this freedom" (p. ix). For many faculty and students in the higher learning, the "search for truth" seems to refer to the freedom to search for "extant knowledge"—to become "learned" rather than a "learner" (inquirer).

3. We certainly incorporate the acquisition of knowledge in our definition, but instead of proposing that knowledge be organized around the conventional triumvirate (humanities, social sciences, sciences), we suggest that knowledge acquisition should be focused on developing expertise in divergent modes of inquiry.

4. In advancing our purpose of a college education, our intent is not to criticize the diversity of institutional missions across our nation's public and private colleges and universities. To the contrary, we believe that many

colleges and universities have embraced commitments—such as civic engagement and community and international service—that are compelling and worthy. Thus, even though many such commitments are not incorporated into our attempt to capture the common ground across our institutions, we appreciate the extraordinary diversity of higher learning in the United States and emphasize that our proposed purpose both allows and encourages institutional variation in mission.

5. Put differently, to *analyze* is to take apart an idea and break it into its constituent parts with surgical precision and to *synthesize* refers to the ability to bring together various parts or elements and unify them in a coherent and meaningful whole. Using metaphors drawn from Native Americans, to analyze is to be a hawk, whereas to synthesize is to be an eagle—with the latter having the ability to see the "big picture." To *interpret* knowledge and information, from the numeric to the literary and the symbolic, is to "make meaning." These three thinking skills—analysis, synthesis, and interpretation—are, from our perspective, at the center of "critical thinking" and are, in turn, central to pursuing ideas with discipline and imagination.

6. Our emphasis on inquiry is reflected in various writings on teaching and learning. To illustrate, Marilyn Cochrane-Smith and Susan Lytle have contributed to recasting K–12 teacher research as "practitioner inquiry," in which they in effect reposition teachers as practitioners engaged in inquiry. See, for example, *Inquiry as Stance: Practitioner Research for the Next Generation* (2009).

Chapter 5 · *Ideas for Developing Inquiry-Driven Learners*

1. During this stage, UW-Madison graduate student Erin Vander Loop provided invaluable insight. We are very grateful for her contribution.

2. The information contained in the description of each initiative was derived from published materials that are posted at each institution's website.

3. What We Believe In, the Five Foci of Learning: http://www.evergreen.edu/about/fivefoci.htm.

4. Academic Program Pages: http://www.evergreen.edu/about/program pages.htm.

5. Academics Overview: http://www.wpi.edu/academics/academics-over view.html.

6. New Century College, Connecting Your Classroom to the World: http://ncc.gmu.edu/.

7. University of Wisconsin-Madison, figs: http://figs.wisc.edu.

8. University of Wisconsin-Madison, Teaching and Learning Excellence: https://tle.wisc.edu/teaching-academy/teaching-academy-strategic-plan.

9. University of Wisconsin, Technology Enterprise Cooperative: http://www.engr.wisc.edu/centers/uw-tec/education.html.

10. Wiscontrepreneur, A Program of the UW-Madison Office of Corporate Relations: http://challenge.wiscontrepreneur.org/contest/faq.

11. Wiscontrepreneur, A Program of the UW-Madison Office of Corporate Relations: http://challenge.wiscontrepreneur.org/contest/faq.

12. St. Olaf College, CURI: http://www.stolaf.edu/academics/curi/.

13. Indiana University at Bloomington, Center for Innovative Teaching and Learning, A Partnership of OVPUE and UITS: http://www.indiana.edu/%7Eteaching/communities/flpindex.shtml.

14. Indiana University at Bloomington, Center for Innovative Teaching and Learning, Faculty Learning Communities: http://citl.indiana.edu/programs/sotl/flc.php.

15. The University of New Mexico, College of Nursing, Critical Thinking Home: http://hsc.unm.edu/consg/critical/.

references

American Association of University Professors. July 30, 2010. "Background Facts on Contingent Faculty." http://www.aaup.org/AAUP/issues/con tingent/contingentfacts.htm.

Anderson, M. (1992). *Imposters in the Temple.* New York: Simon & Schuster.

Aronowitz, S. (2000). *The Knowledge Factory: Dismantling the Corporate University and Creating True Higher Education.* Boston: Beacon Press.

Arum, R. & Roksa, J. (2010). *Academically Adrift: Limited Learning on College Campuses.* Chicago: University of Chicago Press.

Association of American Colleges and Universities. (2007). *College Learning for the New Global Century.* Washington, DC: Association of American Colleges and Universities.

Association of American Colleges and Universities Board of Directors. (1998). "Statement on Liberal Learning." Association of American Colleges and Universities (AACU). http://www.aacu.org/About/statements/liberal _learning.cfm.

Bakewell, S. (2010). *How to Live: A Life of Montaigne in One Question and Twenty Attempts at an Answer.* New York: Other Press.

Barber, B. (1992). *An Aristocracy of Everyone: The Politics of Education and the Future of America.* New York: Oxford University Press.

Barnett, R. T. (2005). "Recapturing the Universal in the University." *Educational Philosophy and Theory* 37 (6), 785-797.

Barr, R. B. & Tagg, J. (1995). "From Teaching to Learning: A New Paradigm for Undergraduate Education." *Change* 27 (6), 13-25.

Bell, D. (1966). *The Reforming of General Education: The Columbia College Experience in Its Natural Setting.* New York: Columbia University Press.

Bennett, W. J. (1984). *To Reclaim a Legacy: A Report on the Humanities in Higher Education.* Washington, DC: National Endowment for the Humanities.

BenShea, N. (2000). *What Every Principal Would Like to Say—and What to Say Next.* Thousand Oaks, CA: Corwin.

Birnbaum, R. & Shushok, F., Jr. (2001) "The 'Crisis' Crisis in Higher Education." In Altbach, P. G., Gumport, P. J. & Johnstone, D. B., eds., *In Defense of American Higher Education*, pp. 59-84. Baltimore: Johns Hopkins University Press.

Blackburn, R., Armstrong, E, Conrad, C., Didham, J. & McKune, T. (1976). *Changing Practices in Undergraduate Education.* Berkeley, CA: Carnegie Council on Policy Studies in Higher Education.

Blanshard, B., ed. (1973). *The Uses of a Liberal Education.* LaSalle, IL: Open Court.

Bloom, A. (1987). *The Closing of the American Mind: How Higher Education Has Failed Democracy and Impoverished the Souls of Today's Students.* New York: Simon & Schuster.

Bloom, B. S., Englehart, M. D., Furst, E. J., Hill, W. H., Krathwohl, D. R., et al. (1956). *Taxonomy of Educational Objectives,* bk. 1, *Cognitive Domain.* New York: David McKay.

Blumenstyk, G. (July 29, 2011). "Big pharma finds a home on campus: As drug companies scale back spending on R&D, academic research takes on financial risk." *Chronicle of Higher Education,* pp. A1, A3–A4.

Bok, D. (1996). *Higher Learning.* Cambridge, MA: Harvard University Press.

Bok, D. (2006). *Our Underachieving Colleges: A Candid Look at How Much Students Learn and Why They Should Be Learning More.* Princeton, NJ: Princeton University Press.

Booth, D. W. & Thornley-Hall, C. (1991). Portsmouth, NH: Heinemann.

Bousquet, M. (2008). *How the University Works: Higher Education and the Low-Wage Nation.* New York: New York University Press.

Boyer, E. L. (1987). *College: The Undergraduate Experience in America.* New York: Harper & Row.

Boyer, E. L. & Levine, A. (1981). *A Quest for Common Learning: The Aims of General Education.* Washington, DC: Carnegie Foundation for the Advancement of Teaching.

Breneman, D. W. (1994). *Liberal Arts Colleges: Thriving, Surviving, or Endangered?* Washington, DC: Brookings Institution.

Brint, S. (2002). "The Rise of the Practical Arts." In S. Brint, ed., *The Future of the City of Intellect,* pp. 231-259. Stanford, CA: Stanford University Press.

Brint, S., Riddle, R., Turk-Bicakci, L. & Levy, C. S. (2005). "From the Liberal Arts to the Practical Arts in American Colleges and Universities: Organizational Analysis and Curricular Change." *Journal of Higher Education* 76 (2), 151-180.

Bronowski, J. (1973). *The Ascent of Man.* Boston: Little, Brown.

Cahn, S. M. (1979). *Education and the Democratic Ideal.* Chicago: Nelson-Hall.

Carnegie Foundation for the Advancement of Teaching. (1977). *Missions of the College Curriculum*. San Francisco: Jossey-Bass.

Carnegie Foundation for the Advancement of Teaching. (1978). *Liberal Education and the Modern University*. Chicago: University of Chicago Press.

Casement, W. (1996). *The Battle of the Books in Higher Education: The Great Canon Controversy*. New Brunswick, NJ: Transaction Publishers.

Cheney, L. V. (1989). *50 Hours: A Core Curriculum for College Students*. Washington, DC: National Endowment for Humanities.

Cheney, L. V. (1992). *Telling the Truth: A Report on the State of the Humanities in Higher Education*. Washington, DC: National Endowment for the Humanities.

Cochrane-Smith, M. & Lytle, S. L. (2009). *Inquiry as Stance: Practitioner Research for the Next Generation*. New York: Teachers College Press.

Cole, J. R. (2009). *The Great American University: Its Rise to Preeminence, Its Indispensable National Role, Why It Must Be Protected*. New York: PublicAffairs.

Commission on the Humanities. (1980). *The Humanities in American Life*. Berkeley: University of California Press.

Confucius. (1998). *The Analects*, vol. 2. Beijing: Foreign Language Teaching and Studies Press. *Congressional Record*, 106 Cong., 2nd sess., 2000, 117, H.R. 4321, pp. 56-65.

Conrad, C. F. (1978). The *Undergraduate Curriculum: A Guide to Innovation and Reform*. Boulder, CO: Westview Press.

Conrad, C. F. & Johnson, J., eds. (2007). *College and University Curriculum: Placing Learning at the Epicenter of Courses, Programs, and Institutions*. Boston: Pearson Custom Publishing.

Conrad, C. F. & Johnson, J. (2008). "Replenishing Liberal Education: Perspectives from the United States." *Educational Studies* 50 (March), 103-118.

Conrad, C. F. & Pratt, A. M. (1981). "Everyman's Undergraduate Curriculum: A Question of Humanistic Context." *Liberal Education* 67, 168-176.

Conrad, C. F. & Wyer, J. C. (1980). *Liberal Education in Transition*. AAHE-ERIC/Higher Education Research Report, no. 3. Washington, DC: American Association for Higher Education.

Cronon, W. (1998). "'Only Connect . . .': The Goals of a Liberal Education." *American Scholar* 67 (4), 73-80.

Darwin, C. (1859). *On the Origin of Species by Means of Natural Selection, or the Preservation of Favoured Races in the Struggle for Life*. London: John Murray.

Delucchi, M. (1997). Liberal Arts Colleges and the Myth of Uniqueness. *Journal of Higher Education* 68 (4), 414-426.

de Montaigne, M. (1877). *Essays of Michel de Montaigne.* Project Gutenberg's *The Essays of Montaigne, Complete.* Retrieved December 14, 2010, from http//:www.gutenberg.org/files/3600/3600-h/3600-h.htm.

Deresiewicz, W. (2008). "The Disadvantages of an Elite Education." *American Scholar* (Summer), 20-31.

Dewey, J. [1916] (1967). *Democracy and Education.* New York: Free Press.

Dewey, J. (1937). "President Hutchins Proposals to Remake Higher Education." *Social Frontier* 22 (3), 104.

Dewey, J. (1938). *Experience in Education.* New York: Macmillan.

Donoghue, F. (2008). *The Last Professors: The Corporate University and the Fate of the Humanities.* New York: Fordham University Press.

D'Souza, D. (1991). *Illiberal Education: The Politics of Race and Sex on Campus.* New York: Free Press.

Duderstadt, J. J. (2000). *A University for the 21st Century.* Ann Arbor: University of Michigan Press.

Dunn, F. (1993). "The Educational Philosophies of Washington, DuBois, and Houston: Laying the Foundations for Afrocentrism and Multiculturalism." *Journal of Negro Education* 62 (1), 24-34.

Einstein, A. & Infeld, L. (1938). *The Evolution of Physics.* New York: Simon & Schuster.

Folbre, N. (2010). *Saving State U: Why We Must Fix Public Higher Education.* New York: New Press.

Fong, B. (2004). "Liberal Education in the 21st Century." *Liberal Education* (Winter), 8-13.

Friedman, T. L. (2007). *The World Is Flat: A Brief History of the Twenty-First Century.* New York: Farrar, Straus & Giroux.

Friedman, T. L. (July 17, 2011). "Global challenges facing America and the role of education in U.S. competitiveness." Keynote address given at the National Governors Association Annual Meeting, Salt Lake City, Utah.

Fuller, T. (1989), ed. *The Voice of Liberal Learning: Michael Oakeshott on Education.* New Haven, CT: Yale University Press.

Gaff, J. G. (1983). *General Education Today.* San Francisco: Jossey-Bass.

Gamson, Z. F. & Associates. (1984). *Liberating Education.* San Francisco: Jossey-Bass.

Gates, H. L., Jr. (1992). *Loose Canons: Notes on the Culture Wars.* New York: Oxford University Press.

Gazzaniga, M. S. (2008). *Human: The Science Behind What Makes Us Unique.* New York: Ecco Books, Harper Collins.

Giamatti, A. B. (1988). *A Free and Ordered Space: The Real World of the University.* New York: W. W. Norton.

Giroux, H. A. (2007). *The University in Chains: Confronting the Military-Industrial-Academic Complex*. Boulder, CO: Paradigm Publishers.

Graff, G. (1992). *Beyond the Culture Wars: How Teaching the Conflicts Can Revitalize American Education*. New York: W. W. Norton.

Great Core Curriculum Debate: Education as a Mirror of Culture, The. (1979). New Rochelle, NY: Change Magazine Press.

Hacker, A. & Dreifus, C. (2010). *Higher Education? How Colleges Are Wasting Our Money and Failing Our Kids—and What We Can Do about It*. New York: Times Books.

Hamilton, E. (1957). *The Echo of Greece*. New York: W. W. Norton.

Hanson, V. D., Heath, J., Thornton, B. (2001). *Bonfire of the Vanities: Rescuing the Classics in an Impoverished Age*. Wilmington, DE: ISI Books.

Harter, S. (2006). "The Challenge of Framing a Problem: What Is Your Burning Question?" In Conrad, C. F. & Serlin, R., eds. *The SAGE Handbook on Research in Education: Engaging Ideas and Enriching Inquiry*, pp. 331-348. Thousand Oaks, CA: SAGE.

Hartley, M. (2003). "'There Is No Way without a Because': Revitalization of Purpose at Three Liberal Arts Colleges." *Review of Higher Education* 27 (1), 75-102.

Harvard Committee. (1945). *General Education in a Free Society: Report of the Harvard Committee*. Cambridge MA: Harvard University Press.

Harvard University Faculty of Arts and Sciences. (2007). *Report of the Task Force on General Education*. Cambridge, MA: Harvard University.

Hersh, R. H. & Merrow, J., eds. (2005). *Declining by Degrees: Higher Education at Risk*. New York: Palgrave Macmillan.

Hirsch, E. D., Jr. (1987). *Cultural Literacy: What Every American Needs to Know*. Boston: Houghton Mifflin.

Hirst, P. H. (1974). *Knowledge and the Curriculum*. London: Routledge & Kegan Paul.

Hirst, P. H. & Peters, R. S. (1970). *The Logic of Education*. London: Routledge & Kegan Paul.

Hutchins, R. M. (1936). *The Higher Learning in America*. New Haven, CT: Yale University Press.

Jacoby, R. (1994). *Dogmatic Wisdom: How the Culture Wars Divert Education and Distract America*. New York: Doubleday.

Kaplan, M. (1980). *What Is an Educated Person? The Decades Ahead*. New York: Praeger.

Kimball, B. A. (1986). *Orators and Philosophers: A History of the Idea of Liberal Education*. New York: Teachers College Press.

Kimball, B. A. (1995). "Toward Pragmatic Liberal Education." In R. Orrill, ed., *The Condition of American Liberal Education*, pp. 3-122. New York: College Entrance Examination Board.

Kirp, D. L. (2003). *Shakespeare, Einstein, and the Bottom Line: The Marketing of Higher Education*. Cambridge, MA: Harvard University Press.

Krathwohl, D. R., Bloom, B., and Masia, B. B. (1999) *Taxonomy of Educational Objectives*, bk. 2, *Affective Domain*. New York: Longman.

Kronman, A. (2007). *Education's End: Why Our Colleges and Universities Have Given Up on the Meaning of Life*. New Haven, CT: Yale University Press.

Lawrence-Lightfoot, S. (2009). *The Third Chapter: Passion, Risk, and Adventure in the 25 Years after 50*. New York: Sara Crichton Books.

Levine, L. W. (1996). *The Opening of the American Mind: Canons, Culture, and History*. Boston: Beacon Press.

Lewis, H. R. (2006). *Excellence without a Soul: How a Great University Forgot Education*. New York: Public Affairs.

London, H. I. (1978). "The Politics of the Core Curriculum." *Change* 10, 11 and 62.

Lucas, C. L. (2006). *American Higher Education: A History*. New York: Palgrave Macmillan.

Lumina Foundation for Education. (2011). *The Degree Qualifications Profile*. Indianapolis, IN: Lumina Foundation for Education.

Martin, J. R. (1994). *Changing the Educational Landscape: Philosophy, Women, and Curriculum*. New York: Routledge.

Martin, W. B. (1982). *College of Character*. San Francisco: Jossey Bass.

Matar, H. (2007). "In the Country of Men." *Goldlink* 28, 10-12.

McGrath, E. J. (1976). *General Education and the Plight of Modern Man*. Indianapolis, IN: Lilly Endowment.

McMahon, W. W. (2009). *Higher Learning, Greater Good: The Private and Social Benefits of Higher Education*. Baltimore: Johns Hopkins University Press.

Menand, L. (2010). *The Marketplace of Ideas: Reform and Resistance in the American University*. New York: W. W. Norton.

Mencken, H. L. (2010). *Mencken on Mencken: A New Collection of Autobiographical Writings*. Baton Rouge: Louisiana State University Press.

Miller, G. E. (1988). *The Meaning of General Education: Emergence of a Curriculum Paradigm*. New York: Teachers College Press.

Mulcahy, D. G. (2008). *The Educated Person: Toward a New Paradigm for Liberal Education*. Lanham, MD: Rowman & Littlefield.

Mulcahy, D. G. (2009). "What Should It Mean to Have a Liberal Education in the 21st Century?" *Curriculum Inquiry* 39 (3), 465-486.

Murchland, B. (1976). "The Eclipse of the Liberal Arts." *Change* 8, 22-26.

National Consumer Law Center Report. (2005). *Making the Numbers Count: Why Proprietary School Performance Data Doesn't Add Up and What Can Be Done about It.* Boston: National Consumer Law Center.

National Educational Alliance. (1940). *The Popular Educator Library: A Liberal Education Standard.* 10 vols. New York: National Education Alliance.

Newfield, C. (2008). *Unmaking the Public University: The Forty-Year Assault on the Middle Class.* Cambridge, MA: Harvard University Press.

Noble, D. F. (2001). *Digital Diploma Mills: The Automation of Higher Education.* New York: Monthly Review Press.

Nussbaum, M. C. (1997). *Cultivating Humanity: A Classical Defense of Reform in Liberal Education.* Cambridge, MA: Harvard University Press.

Nussbaum, M. C. (2010). *Not for Profit: Why Democracy Needs the Humanities.* Princeton, NJ: Princeton University Press.

Oakley, F. (1992). *Community of Learning: The American College and the Liberal Arts Tradition.* New York: Oxford University Press.

O'Connell, B. (2005). *Fifty Years in Public Causes: Stories from a Road Less Traveled.* Medford, MA: Tufts University Press.

Proctor, B. (2007). Foreword. In S. G. Scalese, *The Whisper in Your Heart,* pp. xiii-xiv. 2nd ed. Bloomington, IN: Author House.

Proctor, R. E. (1988). *Education's Great Amnesia: Reconsidering the Humanities from Petrarch to Freud.* Bloomington: Indiana University Press.

Ramaley, J., Leskes, A. & Associates. (2002). *Greater Expectations: A New Vision for Learning as a Nation Goes to College.* Greater Expectations National Panel. Washington, DC: Association of American Colleges and Universities.

Ramo, J. C. (2009). *The Age of the Unthinkable: Why the New World Disorder Constantly Surprises Us and What We Can Do about It.* New York: Little, Brown.

Readings, B. (1996). *The University in Ruins.* Cambridge, MA: Harvard University Press.

Rhodes, T. (2010). "Since We Seem to Agree, Why Are the Outcomes So Difficult to Achieve?" *New Directions for Teaching and Learning* 121 (Spring), 13-21.

Rifkin, J. (2010). *The Empathic Civilization: The Race to Global Consciousness in a World in Crisis.* New York: Penguin.

Rudolph, F. (1962). *The American College and University: A History.* New York: Vintage Books.

Rudolph, F. (1977). *Curriculum: A History of the American Undergraduate Course of Study since 1636.* San Francisco: Jossey-Bass.

Sarchett, B. W. (1995). "What's All This Fuss about This Postmodern Stuff?" In J. Arthur and A. Shapiro, eds., *Campus Wars: Multiculturalism and the Politics of Difference,* pp. 19-27. Boulder, CO: Westview Press.

Schaefer,W. D. (1990). *Education without Compromise: From Chaos to Coherence in Higher Education.* San Francisco: Jossey-Bass.

Schlesinger, A. M., Jr. (1991). *The Disuniting of America: Reflections on a Multicultural Society.* New York: W. W. Norton.

Schmidt, G. P. (1957). *The Liberal Arts College: A Chapter in American Cultural History.* New Brunswick, NJ: Rutgers University Press.

Schön, D. A. (1987). *Educating the Reflexive Practitioner: Toward a New Design for Teaching and Learning in the Professions.* San Francisco: Jossey-Bass.

Schrecker, E. (2010). *The Lost Soul of Higher Education: Corporatization, the Assault on Academic Freedom, and the End of the American University.* New York: New Press.

Shumar, W. (1997). *College for Sale: A Critique of the Commodification of Higher Education.* Washington, DC: Falmer Press.

Slaughter, S. & Leslie, L. L. (1997). *Academic Capitalism: Politics, Policies, and the Entrepreneurial University.* Baltimore: Johns Hopkins University Press.

Slaughter, S. & Rhoades, G. (2004). *Academic Capitalism and the New Economy: Markets, State, and Higher Education.* Baltimore: Johns Hopkins University Press.

Smith, P. (1990). *Killing the Spirit: Higher Education in America.* New York: Viking Penguin.

Smith, P. (2004). *The Quiet Crisis: How Higher Education Is Failing America.* Bolton, MA: Anker.

Solomon, R. C. & Solomon, J. (1993). *Up the University: Re-Creating Higher Education in America.* Reading, MA: Addison-Wesley.

Stewart, D. W. & Spille, H. A. (1988) *Diploma Mills: Degrees of Fraud.* New York: American Council on Education / and Macmillan.

Sullivan, W. M. & M. S. Rosin. (2008). *A New Agenda for Higher Education: Shaping a Life of the Mind for Practice.* San Francisco: Jossey-Bass.

Svaglic, M. J., ed. (1982). *The Idea of a University.* Notre Dame, IN: University of Notre Dame Press.

Thelin, J. R. (2004). *A History of American Higher Education.* Baltimore: Johns Hopkins University Press.

Thomas, R. (1962). *The Search for a Common Learning: General Education, 1800-1960.* New York: McGraw-Hill.

Tierney, W. G. & Hentschke, G. C. (2007). *New Players, Different Game: Understanding the Rise of For-Profit Colleges and Universities.* Baltimore: Johns Hopkins University Press.

Tuchman, G. (2009). *Wannabe U: Inside the Corporate University.* Chicago: University of Chicago Press.

U.S. Bureau of Labor Statistics. December 3, 2001. BLS releases 2000-2010 employment projections. http://www.bls.gov/news.release/history/ecopro _12032001.txt.

U.S. Bureau of Labor Statistics. Employment projections—2008-18. December 10, 2009. http://www.bls.gov/news.release/archives/ecopro_12102009.pdf.

U.S. Department of Education. (2010). Program Integrity: Gainful Employment; Proposed Rule. 34 CFR Part 668. http://edocket.access.gpo.gov /2010/pdf/2010-17845.pdf

U.S. Department of Education Official Cohort Rates Published for Schools Participating in the Title IV Student Financial Assistance Programs. (2009) Retrieved from: www2.ed.gov/offices/OSFAP/default management/cdr.html.

Van Doren, M. (1943). *Liberal Education.* New York: Henry Holt.

van Gelder, R. "Interview with a Best-Selling author: John Steinbeck." *Cosmopolitan* (April, 1947), 123-124.

Veblen, T. (1918). *Higher Learning in America.* New York: Sagamore Press.

Vedder, R. K. (2004). *Going Broke by Degree: Why College Costs Too Much.* Washington, DC: American Enterprise Institute for Public Policy Research.

Veysey, L. R. (1965). *Emergence of the American University.* Chicago: University of Chicago Press.

Wagner, T. (2008). *The Global Achievement Gap.* New York: Basic Books.

Wegner, C. (1978). *Liberal Education and the Modern University.* Chicago: University of Chicago Press.

Welsh-Huggins, A. (February 5, 2010). Leader of Nation's Biggest Campus Taking on Tenure. Associated Press. http://nl.newsbank.com/nl-search /we/Archives?p_product=APAB&p_theme=apab&p_action=search&p _maxdocs=200&s_dispstring=%22smokestacks%20of%20the%20cen tury%22&p_field_advanced-0=&p_text_advanced-0=(%22smokestacks %20of%20the%20century%22)&xcal_numdocs=20&p_perpage=10&p_ sort=YMD_date:D&xcal_useweights=no

Westbrook, R. B. (1991). John Dewey and American Democracy. Ithaca, NY: Cornell University Press.

White, T. H. (1987). *The Once and Future King.* New York: Ace Books.

Wilshire, B. (1990). *The Moral Collapse of the University: Professionalization, Purity, and Alienation.* Albany: State University of New York Press.

Wriston, H. M. (1937). *The Nature of a Liberal College.* Appleton, WI: Lawrence College Press.

index